# The Star Spangled Banner

by

## Barbara Schlichting

Jean!
Enjoy!
Barb Schlichting
5/12/17

## DARKHOUSE BOOKS

THE STAR SPANGLED BANNER
*A First Ladies Mystery*
*by*
*Barbara Schlichting*

*The Star Spangled Banner*

*Copyright © 2016 by Barbara Schlichting*
*ISBN 978-0-9961828-7-4*
*Published May, 2016*
*Published in the United States of America*

*Darkhouse Books*
*160 J Street, #2223*
*Niles, California 94539*

## Table of Contents

# Chapter One

The front window rattled against the wind as I unlocked the door of the First Lady White House Dollhouse store and walked inside toward the dollhouse tables. Dolley Madison and I were distantly related, so greeting her first seemed natural.

I wore a new pink dress to match Dolley's inaugural gown. After two months of interest in several White House dollhouses for her national chain store's toy department, Jackie Newell, was coming to get a firsthand look. She was scheduled to arrive within the hour, which left me with just enough time to spruce up the showroom and ensure that my 1814 White House dollhouse arrangement was in perfect shape. This was my chance to make the big time.

"There, there, now Dolley." I straightened her because she'd tipped slightly. "Mr. Prez? You need to be on your best behavior today. No chasing Dolley around the house with my perspective buyer coming soon! No pinching her bum." I wagged my finger at him.

"Mrs. Lincoln? You're looking marvelous today. How's the headache after that awful carriage ride? It was an attempt on your life, wasn't it?" I'd had an awful one after the car accident that killed my parents when I was eleven. Now, it's an ache in my heart, still—twenty years later.

I glanced over to the First Lady pictures hanging on the wall.

"Why are you crooked, Barbara?" I stopped to straighten the first Mrs. Bush's portrait.

"I'll return shortly to fix your hair."

"Mrs. Carter, I hope last night was worth it. All that Billy Beer." Something isn't right. Mrs. Carter has never been this tipsy.

"Don't worry, ladies, you're back to looking good."

I winked while passing.

Near the backroom, I gasped at a crunch underfoot. Another step. Another crunch. I gazed across the hallway floor, and the bottom sank from my stomach. My eyes opened wide, I'd walked across broken furniture.

"Hello?" I flicked on the light in the workroom. Boxes and boxes lay strewn across the floor. Miniature chairs, tables, dolls, vases, desks, and beds were scattered. The workbench was littered with broken dollhouse pieces. My sewing items were tossed about.

I screamed.

I was sure that it reached the psychic shop next door. Mikal, the proprietor, kept his window open for fresh air.

I heard a noise, as I began backing out toward the bathroom. Meaty, strong arms came from behind and covered my mouth, pulling me against a firm chest. I smelled a slight vanilla scent as I bit into the assailant's fleshy fingers. I struggled, biting harder, trying to stomp his feet, but he held tight.

Grandpa's open toolbox full of hammers, nails, and box cutters lay almost within reach. I tried inching closer, but my captor jerked my head back, clutching my hair. I twisted to see him. A black ski mask covered his face.

"NO screaming." His icy tone sent fear up my spine. "You hear?" He slowly brought down his hand after I tried to nod.

"Where are they?" He wrenched my left arm up behind my back. Pain seared up my arm, as I leaned closer to the toolbox. "I want them now."

"Ouch! You're hurting me!"

"Where are they?"

"You're breaking my arm." He loosened his grip. "I'm not psychic here. Just tell me what you want." Slowly I moved my right hand while inching closer to the toolbox. "I don't understand." I grabbed a box cutter from the workbench and quietly snapped it open. "My fiancé is a cop, so—."

"Shut up!"

The toolbox tumbled over, sending its contents skittering across the floor. My assailant's hand loosened from my back, giving me enough time to turn and thrust the blade into his forearm. He yelped and grabbed at his bleeding arm.

I dashed out the back door. "Help!" Scrambling down the alley and rounding the building to the front of the store, I screamed again then ducked inside the doorway of Mikal's shop.

"Liv, calm down. What's wrong?" Mikal walked toward me with a client following. "Another mouse?" He grinned and glanced at his client. "Stephanie, my neighbor, Liv."

"I don't have time for this stupidity," I said.

"Excuse me!" Stephanie said. The short, stocky client peeked out from behind Mikal, narrowed her eyes and crossed her arms over her flat chest. "Listen, missy. I was in the middle of a reading. It was just getting good! I found out about my husband's little girlie friend with the big boobs. Now this!" She threw her arms in the air. "My reading is botched. I want a refund."

"You haven't paid." Mikal glared at her.

"I won't either." She marched away, but not before giving me the finger.

"Hey! I'm in trouble, loser! I was assaulted just now." Just because I'd evicted a live-in mouse family from my shop a few weeks ago didn't mean it was back. "Someone trashed my shop and grabbed me." I pulled my cell phone from my pocket and called Aaron, my fiancé.

"Sit down, right here," Mikal ordered. "I'm calling the cops."

My boyfriend picked up the call. "Aaron, someone just attacked me at the shop." I sank into the chair.

"Are you hurt? What happened?"

"I'm fine, I'm at Mikal's."

"I'll be right there," Aaron said. "Have you called 911?"

"No, I called you."

"I'll take care of it, then I'll be right there." Aaron disconnected.

"I'm going back. The Gorilla must be gone by now." I took a deep breath and headed for the door.

"Stay and wait for Aaron," Mikal urged.

"Nope. I've got to check on the store." I had to protect the ladies. The First Ladies had already been through so much in their life, now it's up to me to make sure nothing else happens to them. Mommy always said they were special, like being the Nation's Mother. As First Lady, she'd make sure that the President looked out for our interests and needs like food for the hungry.

"I'll stay outside, I promise."

I texted my best friend, Maggie, as I walked out the door. My knees felt weak, like I might sink to the ground. *Where were the police?* My feet crunched in the snow, and I started to shiver. I could've been badly hurt. *Where was Aaron?* My arm ached as I massaged it, trying to ignore the pain. *Was the man gone or still in the store? What did he mean? Where are they? Where's what?*

I stood to the side to wait.

Where was Max?

Max worked part-time for me and rented the apartment above the shop. He should be around here someplace, but who knows? Max often gambled away his money. I was always getting cryptic messages from parts unknown, asking how to reach him, presumably to remove body parts.

A reassuring chuckle from behind made me grin. Max's voice boomed from above. "Livvie! Now what? Another mouse in the house?"

My headache suddenly grew to the size of Texas. I glanced up and massaged my temples.

"Someone broke in, and assaulted me. The workroom's a mess." Tears streamed down my cheeks. I wiped my nose with the sleeve of my heavy sweater just as Aaron's squad car drove up.

Aaron's smile made my toes curl. I knew that I could make through this day.

Tim, Aaron's partner, went around to the back while Aaron stayed out front.

Finally, sirens blared in the distance and soon stopped. Two police officers climbed from the car, as Aaron and Tim secured the premises. People gathered to stare at the building while other shopkeepers popped out to gawk.

"Everyone move on and go about their business. Now!" Aaron said.

Max walked down the outside steps. He gave me a puzzled look, lit a smoke, and stood near me as an officer approached us.

"You the owner?" the officer stated.

"Yes."

"You?" he turned to Max.

"He's my upstairs renter and employee." I noticed two plain-clothes officers approaching, one older with gray hair, the other younger and blond.

"We'll take over. There's been a rash of burglaries in the area," the detective stated, showing his badge. "Detective Mergens. Ms. Anderson? Olivia Anderson? You called it in?"

"My fiancé called it in, but I'm Olivia, Liv, Anderson."

"Ms. Anderson," he said. "My partner, Detective Erlandsen, and I, are curious about this theft because of its nature."

"Yes, let's go inside for some privacy," Detective Erlandsen said.

"I'll follow." My phone buzzed, and I read Maggie's message, "Stay safe. Keep me updated." The showroom appeared unscathed. I took a deep breath and looked toward the historical White House and saw Dolley. I breathed relief, knowing it was unharmed. The other houses appeared unscathed, but I'd check on the Ladies as soon as possible. *Hold on girls, I'm coming.*

"How does the showroom look?" Mergens asked.

"Great, actually. This morning is very important to me." I stuck my hands in my pockets and went back to the front window.

"Jackie Newell of *Jackie of New York!* Department Store is due here in less than an hour." I shook from deep inside.

"Who?" Mergens asked.

"She is the owner of the national department store chain, *Jackie of New York!*. You know, from the Home Shopping Network."

"Oh! My wife would probably know," Mergens said, rolling his eyes.

"I hope her interest in the houses will spike sales."

"The back lock was picked," Erlandsen stated. "Know anyone who'd want to break in? Have anything valuable in here besides dollhouses?"

"Plenty. Look around the room. I have my Penny Dolls and First Lady photos, and they sell for several hundred dollars, at least." I nodded at them, placing my hands on my hips. We stood by the glass counter in front of the register and computer. I swung my attention back to the officer's question, and crossed my arms. "Max carves doll heads in here or his apartment at night. He sets his own hours. I tell him what style of house I need and which First Lady. The pieces need to be glued and, in some instances, stapled together. They're fragile, but sturdy. He fills in when needed."

"You trust him?" Mergens asked.

"Absolutely. He has a key. He lives here. I've known him for years." I crossed my arms. "His workbench is in the workroom— underneath all that wreckage."

"I see." Mergens wrote in his notepad. "Was he home?"

"I don't know."

"Where do you live?"

"With my grandparents, Marie and August Ott." I scratched my head. "I've never given Dorrie a key. She's my other employee."

"Any cause for alarm?" He studied me. "You know. Anything unusual. Pattern change such as misplacing a key?"

"We want this Dorrie's info," Erlandsen said.

"I can't think of anything unusual at the moment." I shook my head. "I keep my purse in the workroom, and it's usually hung on the clothes tree." I quickly looked up Dorrie's contact information from the list beside the computer. "Here's her info. I'm sure it was a man because of his strength and low voice. Now can I see the damage?" I became more worried with each passing minute.

"Anything you can tell me about the guy who attacked you?" Detective Mergens cocked his head. "It's pretty nasty in there. We thought we'd get all the information before you see it." He frowned. "It'll be a shock."

"I saw some of it before he grabbed me." I sank into the nearest chair and reached for the tissue box. I thought of Jackie Kennedy and all the pain she'd endured as I wiped my nose. "He was big. A gorilla. HUGE. His fingers and hands were beefy. His biceps pumped up when he tightened his grip on me. He wore a ski mask. His voice sounded like it had potholes and icebergs." I glanced at the clock and suddenly my brain kicked into gear. "Can we hustle here? I'm expecting a very important client pretty soon." I blew my nose.

"One more question." Erlandsen held up a finger. "Anyone you might have a beef with?"

"I can't think of anyone." I frowned, massaging my chin. "Unless this has something to do with Max. He gambles and often loses." I thought a moment. "The beefy guy asked, where are they? I don't know what he was talking about. Where is what?"

"He was after something in particular. Now, we're getting somewhere. That's more than what the other victims could tell us." Erlandsen glanced up at me.

"What other victims?" I stared at him. "I'm not the first?"

"There's been a rash with break-ins," Erlandsen said. "Ongoing investigation."

"Dollhouses?" I asked. I glanced at each detective. "Good grief. This doesn't make sense. I'll keep a closer watch."

They closed their notepads.

"Now are we done?" I asked. "I've plenty to do."

"Almost." Erlandsen stepped aside. "We're in the process of checking for prints."

I waited a beat, my stomach tied in knots, as the door opened and closed. They left. I got up and forced myself to go to the workroom, stopping just outside the doorway. My gaze swept across the floor of the workroom. *The poor first ladies. Broken china dishes. Pieces scattered from one end of the room to the other. Poor Mrs. Monroe with the French furniture.* Tears streamed down my cheeks. It'd take hours to sort through everything and decide what was salvageable.

"What a mess. It's a disaster," I whispered. "What were they after? Will they be back?"

I went into the restroom, glanced in the tiny mirror, fluffed up my hair, dabbed on some red lipstick, and noticed a chipped nail. A file was handy and soon the chipped nail was smooth. *Hopefully, I look presentable for Jackie Newell's arrival.* The back door opened just as I stepped from the bathroom.

"Hey, babe." Aaron walked toward me. "Don't worry about a thing. I've requested a few days off but don't know for sure if it'll be approved. I also wouldn't be surprised is if the sarge calls me in for a half shift. We're short officers right now due to the flu season."

"Thank you." The front bell jingled.

"I'll call you later." Aaron tweaked my chin. "By the way, I put a box of chocolate under the register."

"Another, among many reasons why I love you," I said.

He left.

I tried to calm my nerves by taking deep breaths.

Aaron stepped back in. "Don't forget to call the insurance agent."

"Already on my to-do list."

He walked to his patrol car and drove away. I noticed a familiar car parked out back, and realized that it belonged to an old schoolmate, Ronnie. He earned his living by taking pictures and writing news articles for the local paper. I cringed.

I went to the register, slipped off the box cover and removed two chocolate pieces, stuffing both in my mouth. A third piece sounded good, so I shoved it into my mouth before setting the box under the register. A car door slammed and I went to the front window.

A long, black limousine was parked in front of the store. Jackie Newell and a thirtyish woman climbed out, followed by a big, burly man wearing aviator sunglasses and a black suit. I figured him as a bodyguard or escort.

"You can do this," I told myself, gulping. Opening the front door, I willed my racing heart to slow down. "Good morning."

Both women stood about the same height. Ms. Newell wore a ritzy black dress coat and the younger woman was dressed in a simple navy suit. Ms. Newell's practiced smile shone as she walked toward the store, the other woman following two paces behind. The bodyguard had his eyes glued on the passersby. *Why does she need a bodyguard?* I swept the hair back from my face, smiling.

"Ms. Newell, I hope that you'll like the store." I pretended as if all was well as my fast beating heart slowed to a normal pace. I jutted my hand out. "Olivia Anderson, but you can call me Liv."

"Call me Jackie. So nice to meet you." She shook my hand before glancing around the room. "Very nice. Yes, indeed. Love your pictures of the First Ladies. Who is your favorite?"

"Dolley, of course."

The woman beside Jackie cleared her throat.

"My secretary, Wanda Brown. She's invaluable. Don't know what I'd do without her." Jackie gave a winning smile.

Calm my pumping heart. Yes! Maybe a dozen or more houses purchased by her highness.

Wanda held out her hand. "Nice to meet you." Her eyes shifted around the room. "Nice store you have."

"Thank you."

Jackie's eyes lingered on the heritage-style White House.

"I see you have Dolley Madison as the First Lady in this house." Jackie tucked her small pouch under her arm before reaching into the house. "May I?" She picked up the doll and began examining it. "Tell me about the gown. It's gorgeous. I see it's layered with crinolines and even has pantaloons."

"I sew the clothing with as much authenticity as possible." I smiled. "The dress Mrs. Madison is wearing is representative of what she wore for the Inaugural Ball. It's made of buff-colored velvet with ropes of pearls and a fashionable turban with Bird of Paradise flowers. She was the first to have an Inaugural Ball. Leave it to Dolley."

I spoke with confidence. I had studied the First Ladies in college, read the history books as well as the gossipy ones. I could have entertained Jackie all day with my grasp on White House minutiae, but I wasn't sure if she was an enthusiast like me.

"Very informative." Jackie's eyes lit up as she gave the doll a closer inspection. "I hear you're a descendant of Dolley Madison."

"Yes, I am, as a matter of fact." I glanced outside. Max was passing by with a cup in one hand and a bag in the other. "Are you?"

"I am as well. She's amazing."

"Who's your favorite?"

Wanda was also watching Max pass by, and a smile crossed her lips. Go figure.

"Dolley too." Jackie grinned. "It's beautiful." She carefully placed the piece back in its original position. "Ever hear of the family secret?" She removed a magnifying glass from her purse and knelt down to peer closely at the interior walls.

"A family secret? No. Never heard of it." I furrowed my brows.

"Are you certain?" Jackie eyed me suspiciously.

"Yes." I nodded. *What is she talking about?*

"Most interesting." She looked me square in the eye.

Is she trying to figure out if I'm telling the truth?

"How long have you known you're a descendant?" I returned her stare.

"Last year. I've done plenty of research into it. There's definitely a family secret," she said. "Back to business." Ms. Newell straightened up. "Are the wall decorations identical to how Dolley decorated?"

"What do you mean?" I asked, raising a brow. "Of course they are! The wall hanging is quite similar to my grandma's."

"Gorgeous." Wanda leaned closer to Jackie. She held up china from the Madison house.

The bell jingled. The bodyguard entered and stood in front of the door. He crossed his arms. "Problem solved."

Wanda nodded.

What is he talking about? Problem solved?

These people from New York seemed to talk in riddles, or else I was losing it. This conversation is giving me the jitters. I glanced across the street to the park. When Wanda cleared her throat, it jerked me back to attention.

"She's concerned about historical accuracy." Wanda looked me in the eye. "She's interested in all things Dolley, including Mr. Madison."

"No family rumor or 'secret' heard of, eh?" Jackie stood and dropped the magnifier into her little purse. She glanced at me once again. "Sure?"

"Positive."

"Is every adornment on the clothing accurately portrayed on both Mr. and Mrs. Madison?" Jackie asked.

"She wants to know if this is exactly what was worn during the inaugural ball," Wanda clarified.

"Yes. Dolley's dress. Everything on it is accurate as well as his, but his is purchased. Men's clothing is very tough to sew." *What is with the tag team between the two?*

"I'm interested in a 'secret', but if you don't know of one—," Jackie said.

"I don't." I shook my head. *What is with her? What secret?* I had to change the subject to get back in control. "All the dollhouses are made by hand. I have two employees, one who carves the dolls' heads and my showroom assistant who helps arrange the interior settings." *Isn't she going to purchase a few houses?*

Jackie held up President Madison and scrutinized his cufflinks. I blinked.

"Mr. Madison's cufflinks have been missing from the duPont museum for years. You know? Montpelier? The Madison home? It's part of the 'secret,' my dear." She cocked her brow and stared right through me. "They need finding."

"I don't know what you're talking about," I said, running my fingers through my hair. "I know the duPont's purchased the estate some years after it was sold by Dolley."

"Excuse me," Wanda interrupted. "You have thirty minutes until you're scheduled to meet with Mr. Carlson." Wanda looked at me. There was something in her eyes, but I wasn't sure what. Curiosity? "We're booked at the Twin City Hotel. It makes getting around easy. Only a couple blocks from here."

"May I take Mr. and Mrs. Madison with me today for further scrutiny? I'll place my order on Wednesday and then return them. Day after tomorrow." Jackie opened her little pouch and dropped the dolls inside before I could say, "Boo."

"Wait a second, here. I need a credit card number." I was beginning to think she was a magician, the way she made those dolls disappear.

"Here." Wanda handed me the card.

"I'll make out the sale, but hold the charge until they're returned." I took care of the paper work before they left, leaving me confused. "How many houses do you think you'll purchase? I'd like to know so that they'll be ready."

"Maybe two heritage houses, but I'm not sure."

At the window, I watched them leave, Jackie with her purse tucked tight under her arm like a million dollar bank vault. First Jackie, then Wanda climbed into the car. The bodyguard held the door open, shutting it behind.

What family secret?

# Chapter Two

Persuading my grandparents over a short phone call that I wasn't injured except my pride proved harder than I'd hoped. Aaron, who lived next door, had already told them about the assault. They tried to convince me to close the store for the day, but I wanted alone time to peruse the out of jail or suspended sentence prisoner lineup page for Hennepin County. After a short while, I found it. Ten men appeared tall and meaty, just like the gorilla, but how would I know for sure? I wrote the suspect names down on a sheet of paper with the intention of later a later information search. I glanced at the clock, only to realize that too much time had slipped by. I had work to do. I popped a CD into the player, and the day sped by. As I worked, I wondered if there had been a meeting at the Foshay Tower between Ms. Newell and Mr. Carlson?

"Mrs. Roosevelt, keep your eye on Teddy. He's looking peeked from his travels," I said. I stood near the modern house. It appeared as if Michelle Obama winked so I returned one. "Mrs. Eisenhower, you look simply smashing today in pink." I glanced around at the ladies. "Good night, all!"

I surveyed the workroom. Several boxes still needed sorting. The fabric for making the gowns was destroyed, and I made a mental note to order more. Dorrie could continue the sorting.

I called my best friend Maggie before leaving. I told her about the dolls and the question of the family secret.

"If I were you, I'd be extra careful. Nothing sounds right," Maggie said.

"I know."

"I'm still raising the question that I've asked for years, why doesn't your grandma know the reason behind the flag in the corner of the sampler?"

"The sampler embroidered by Dolley has always been a puzzle," I said. "I sifted through Hennepin county files and recorded ten names."

"Your likely suspects? Liv, leave to the professionals. You're almost married to a cop, let Aaron look into it." Maggie waited a beat. "I'd be more interested in the family secret. What in the world would that be?"

"I'd like to know the answer, also. I'll talk to you later."

I disconnected while growing ever more curious as I headed out to the car and the drive home.

One summer vacation, my parents took me to Washington, D.C. Dad had a hard time peeling Mom and me away from the First Lady exhibit. As a young girl, I loved dolls and selling dollhouses and First Ladies seemed a natural step. It helped me keep Mom's memory alive.

I planned to shower and grab a bite to eat. My phone dinged with a text from Aaron.

*I'll help tonight at the store. Don't worry. We'll assemble houses and you won't be alone.*

I felt better.

> *Good,* I replied. *We'll get everything ready for the next go round with Jackie.*

Jackie's question about a "secret" still gnawed at me. *What did she mean? Is the answer in front of me? Why take the dolls? What's all this about the cufflinks?*

In the living room, I studied Grandma's sampler wall hanging. The embroidered motifs were so even and neat, stitched in the Quaker style. The flag on the upper right corner always perplexed me, as it did Maggie, because each of the other three corners had a marigold. Four unaligned strawberries along both sampler sides were stitched, but the thirteen strawberries at the bottom and top were unaligned. Each of the strawberries had thirteen gold seeds made of tiny French knots. The sampler center was sparse, except for four gold French knots, which appeared to divide the sampler into quarters.

The sampler struck me as odd. I always thought there was some kind of secret message hidden in it when I looked at it. *Secret? Are there more unknown samplers?*

*Are the samplers some sort of roadmap to the unknown secret? It has to be my imagination.*

I turned away and glanced at the First Lady dolls in the cabinet, which stood on the back wall. I stared at the Dolley doll. "Are you trying to tell me something?"

"Here you are." Aaron came beside me and draped his arm over my shoulders. "Why do the strawberries jump up and down, I wonder?"

"No clue. I've always wondered why the corner flag, with the other three corners as marigolds? Dolley must've had a reason at the time." I looked up at him, and we kissed.

"Ready?"

"Ready as I can be. We have our work cut out for us. Thanks for taking the shift off to help assemble the houses and for putting in new door locks. There's so much to be done. Max is busy carving the doll heads, and I've already assembled the body parts. Thank heavens Jackie didn't take any more than the two dolls. I did get a credit card, and she said that she'd return them. It's all very confusing. Just like the day was. It's plain weird like. Bodyguard? I don't get it." *Quit babbling.*

"Huh? Dolls? Tell me later," he said, running his fingers through my hair. "What's this about? Bodyguard? You're confusing me."

"See? I'm confused. Everything about her is strange." I frowned. "Max is almost finished carving Mr. Madison's head. I hope to spend tomorrow finishing whatever we don't get done tonight." I leaned into him. "All we can do is hope for the best."

"I agree, curly top. Grab your bag and let's go." Aaron steered me away from Grandma's doll cabinet. "She ordered two houses, you say? Good thing all of the wood pieces weren't broken."

"Yeah, not to mention the china dishes, lamps, and some other stuff. The intruder hadn't reached the boxes of newer inventory."

Grandma and Grandpa waved us over as we passed the door to the recently added sunroom, which was complete with the indoor whirlpool I had talked them into purchasing. I knew we'd find them in there, drinking their favorite sodas and playing cards.

"Who's winning?" I asked, entering.

"I am, of course," Grandma said. She gazed up at me through thick glasses and smiled.

I always thought Grandma was cute. She'd shrunk to a mere five-feet-one, and her sea-green eyes always had a glint in them. Her upturned mouth appeared as if she wore a perpetual smile. She had small hands and feet. Her hair came to her neck, and she'd wear it either tied back in a ponytail or wound up in a bun. For some reason she never wore it straight. Her hair color had faded from black to silver-gray.

"You're going to stay with her, aren't you?" Grandpa set his glass of Sprite down. "Wouldn't want another intruder breaking in. The next time, she might not be as lucky." He narrowed his brow and stared at Aaron. "You're a cop. Protect her."

"Yes, August. I'll do my best." Aaron pulled me closer. "I'll stay right by her side."

"Will you be back tonight?" Grandma sipped her root beer.

"We've got plenty to do. I'll probably stay at Aaron's if we do come back." I leaned over and gave them each a peck on the cheek. "I'll call later."

"Good night." Aaron took my hand and pulled me along to his car. "I love your grandparents. August keeps me on my toes." Aaron grinned as he waited for me to climb inside.

"They've been married for so many years and are still in love. I hope we can be the same way." I climbed inside the van and buckled up. "My parents would have been married fifty years if they were still alive."

"Yeah, mine too. I still believe that Dad died from a broken heart when Mom passed away. Damn ovarian cancer. No siblings because of it, neither of us." Before starting the car, he leaned over and gave me a smooch and turned on the radio.

"I glanced through the former prisoner page for Hennepin County and came up with ten names."

"Give it to me, and I'll do what I can, but you have to promise to keep your nose from police business," Aaron said. "Promise?"

"Promise."

After driving past Howe Elementary School, we headed toward downtown, making our way across the Hennepin Avenue Bridge.

Aaron parked behind the store, right beside Max's old pickup.

I wasn't looking forward to the long evening, but time was running short. "Here we go, and it's already six o'clock," I said.

We entered through the back door.

"How's it going?" I found Max bent over the workbench, carving a head. Piles of wood shavings spread across the newspapers covering the workbench. "Dolley?"

"Yep. She's harder to do because of the twinkle in her eyes."

"I can believe it." I swept and filled empty boxes with the items that had been strewn across the floor. The waning evening sunlight cast shadows across my sewing machine and table in the corner by a window. Thankfully, my pincushion, scissors, and thimble sat undisturbed.

"Phone's been ringing off the hook." Max glanced from me to Aaron and then back again. "Sure hope we can get a lot done."

"Who's called?"

"Reporters. Maybe a customer or two asking about hours." Max looked at me. "You okay?"

"Yep. There's a lot riding on this, such as your paycheck and my month's rent." I stared at him. "Jackie Newell is eager to get those houses, remember? We'll manage." I put on some of my favorite tunes.

"I need concentration. Facial lines are hard to get right. I'm turning down the tunes," Max said.

"This way, honey," I said to Aaron.

"Let's see," Aaron said, picking up a marked box. "It's house pieces."

"Follow me. We can do the gluing on the computer counter." We walked together into the showroom. "Hi, ladies. We're back to work so don't disturb us with all of your chattering."

"You're funny, Liv." Aaron grinned. "Do you think he'll be able to get all those heads carved?" Aaron set the box down on the countertop. "How are we going to do this?" He looked around at all the dollhouses. "There's no empty space." He scratched his chin as he walked over to the early 1800 vintage houses and looked inside. "Jackie Newell took the Madison dolls? That's crazy. Did she say why?"

"Not really. It's all a puzzle." I looked at him. "She slipped them into her purse. I caught her at it, and asked for the credit card number. I did make a transaction and promised to hold the charge until they're returned. It was all weird."

"You're right. It is weird. You're a professional. So are they." Aaron began taking care of the pieces. "Some people," Aaron shook his head, "there's no figuring."

I busied myself by arranging pieces in order for gluing, such as the corners and stacking of the walls. We'd glued houses together before, so we had a workable order to follow. Exterior renovations over the years added more features and factors to consider when gluing, but for now we only had to worry about the historical White House of the 1800s.

It seemed like we stood for hours arranging and gluing pieces. The time slipped by as we discussed Jackie Newell.

"Hey, guys," Max called. "I'm leaving. Takin' the stuff with me upstairs." Each head took anywhere from three to four hours to carve, depending on the intricacies of the facial lines, and he still had a ways to go. "I'm having trouble concentrating. Best if I leave."

"We may end up flopping in your living room. Okay?"

"Sure. Just text me a warning first."

"Right." The sudden silence and the closing of the back door caught our attention. "Let's go back to the workroom. Now that he's gone, the shavings and dust shouldn't be a problem with the glue," I said. Aaron followed me to the back.

"I think he's worried about getting them right. The accuracy of facial lines," I said, entering the workroom. "When Max is done with those heads, I have to paint them and they have to dry. I'm already worn out."

"So am I." Aaron shoved aside miscellaneous items and set the box of dollhouse components down on the workbench.

We set to work, sorting and dividing pieces into two platforms. By three a.m., both of us were exhausted, but we'd glued the basic structures together. I was ready to attach the inner walls with my glue gun. We'd use furniture from the unopened shipment that had arrived the day before, and I planned to set Dorrie to the task of furnishing the rooms. I'd dress the dolls after sewing the gowns. I was certain we had plenty of undergarments, even though the fabric for the gowns had been ruined.

"Let's take a break. I need to sleep a few hours. How about you?"

Aaron's eyes drooped. "Good idea."

I was so tired that my brain had turned to mush.

Hating to drive home only to return within a short time, I texted Max, knowing he'd probably be sleeping.

"I've put a call through to the insurance agent, but she hasn't returned my call. I'll have to make a reminder call, I suspect." I'd suddenly thought of it. "I was surprised that two plain detectives came."

"Yes, there's been an awful of lot petty crimes lately, but this one seemed slightly different. That's why."

"They said as much." I waited a minute, and said, "This morning. The assault. The man kept asking, 'Where is it?' Then Jackie asked about a 'secret'. What secret?"

"Why would you first be asked about where something is, as well as questioned about a Madison family secret? It's like two separate cases."

"I agree, and she did say something about cufflinks."

"Cufflinks and a 'secret'? How confusing," Aaron said.

We locked up and headed up the back steps to the apartment, using my key to let us in. I had the extra since I owned the building. We fell asleep on Max's couch and chair.

The morning blast of rap tunes woke us. I rubbed the sand from my eyes and tried to focus. I nudged Aaron, still asleep in the overstuffed chair. In the bathroom, Max turned on the shower.

"Let's get out of here." I nudged Aaron once again and he pried his eyes open.

"Geez, my back hurts." Aaron grimaced as he massaged his lower back.

"Mine aches too."

"What a night. We should've gone home." Aaron glanced at his cell phone. "It's eight. How about if you open the store and get things rolling, while I go pick up some coffee and bagels?"

"Only if it's a double espresso. Better yet, make it a triple." I got up and went to the bathroom door and hollered inside, "Thanks, Max. We're leaving. See you when you come down."

Once inside the store, I called Dorrie to ask if she'd come in early to help. I needed everyone on the job if I wanted to pull this sale off quickly. Time would be tight. Thank heavens for Max's loyalty, but I did pay him plenty.

"Hi ladies," I said inside of the showroom. "I hope you all had a great night."

I went to the workroom.

I set about to put the final touches on the walls. Fortunately, the interior walls were purchased already decorated. All that needed finishing on the walls was setting candles in the wall sconces. Pictures, such as George Washington's portrait, were already painted where they hung. When Aaron returned, I took a short break to freshen up. I couldn't meet with prospective clients looking and smelling the way I did.

"Take a look." Aaron opened the morning newspaper to a headline that read, "*Jackie of New York!*, the Home Shopping network diva, visits our Fair City." The photo caption stated, "After spending time perusing dollhouses, Jackie Newell stood beside the statue of Mary Tyler Moore."

"Look really close at the pictures." Aaron held the paper so I could see.

"Don't tell me." I stared closely at the smaller photos and there it was, me teary eyed, waiting for the police. "What an awful picture." I sipped my coffee, which helped me wake up. I took a bite of my blueberry bagel. "We've got a long day ahead of us."

"It's actually kind of funny." Aaron spread cream cheese on his bagel. "Look at the publicity you're getting."

"True. Still, I won't make any profits if I don't get in gear." I finished my bagel and stood up. "Time to get moving. The shop's been closed for too long."

I set to work. While Aaron worked on the walls, I sifted through the broken pieces, searching for the arm to a rocking chair. Sometime later the door opened.

"Who's there?" I stepped from the workroom and peered into the showroom and saw a customer enter.

"You open for business?" she questioned. "I can return later if that would be better."

"Are you interested in any particular house?"

"Betty Ford," she said.

"Coming right up," I said. "I'll be right there." I turned to Aaron and showed him where the house was and the box with all the items, which I had him tuck under my arm.

"Here's the interior pieces," I said, setting it on the counter. "Someone will be out with the house. I'll have to fetch the dolls, yet." I looked at her and asked, "How will you pay?"

"Credit card," she said, handing it over. "Oh my, here he comes."

I looked over my shoulder at Aaron, and smiled.

"Your car?" he asked.

"Right outside," she answered and quickly signed her name to the receipt. "Follow me."

I heard the back door open, and figured it was Dorrie. "Dorrie," I called.

"What?"

"Bring out Mr. and Mrs. Ford, please."

By the time I'd cleared the register and walked around the counter to carry the box out, Dorrie had arrived with the dolls. Together we carried them out to the car.

"Thanks," I said.

"Came at the right time." Dorrie's lips sparkled as did her eyelids. The nose stud made her resemble a genie in a bottle. Her gold dangly earrings shone like the solar system. Were the spheres miniature planets? Her necklace was a peace sign.

We walked back inside. I turned back to sorting and digging for lost furniture parts as Aaron continued with the houses. I was lucky to have Dorrie working for me because she was good with customers and always on time. We'd known each other since we were kids. I always invited her to parties. She'd stolen once from me when we were kids, then returned the bracelet with the excuse she'd wanted to wear it on a date. That was a very long time ago, and not an issue.

My cell rang. The insurance agent, Margo, said she'd come out later today or tomorrow so I could file the claim. Since I most likely hadn't had a chance to go through the inventory, she could use the police report and pictures when she made out her report.

The day went by fast. Aaron was called back to work. I barely poked my nose out of the workroom all day. Dorrie took care of customers and managed to sort through some of the furniture. Sometime mid-afternoon, Max and Dorrie snuck away. I pretended not to notice. Pink-cheeked and humming, Dorrie returned alone and set to work without making a comment.

"You're missing an earring." I chuckled.

"It must've fallen off when—,"

The back door opened and Max walked in, holding the newly carved doll heads.

"All set. Just need paint." He delicately set the Dolley heads on the workbench.

"Did ya find the prezzes?"

"Nope. Been busy assembling houses along with sewing the clothing. Would you get them, please?" I held my breath and looked away.

"Sure, but we need to talk." He swung the ladder around and stepped on it. He brought down the small wooden box and handed it over.

I raised the lid and smiled. "They're perfect. Now all I need is Mr. Madison's cufflinks for completion, but I know where they are." The recently delivered box was stored on a wall shelf near the sewing machine. "You did great work on those doll heads, and you'll get a bonus, don't worry. I've got an awful lot on my mind. Between the assault and now getting ready for Jackie, it's almost too much. Can't it wait?"

"I realize all of that, but I have something to show you."

We both turned toward Dorrie as she entered, holding another box to sort.

"Am I, ah, interrupting something?" Her pink blush now traveled down her neck and into her bosom.

"You can tell me now."

"We have to talk, but now is not the time." Max jutted out his jaw and strutted away. *What on earth does he want?* The back door closed with a bang.

I cranked my head back to Dorrie.

"I get to ride around in a limo tonight," she said, and sneezed.

"Really? A limo?" I asked.

"I forgot to do something." She cleared her throat.

"I'm sorry. What were you saying?"

"Never mind, it slipped my mind. It's almost closing time. Can I go?"

"You bet. It's been a long day. Enjoy your evening."

By the time six rolled around, all that was left to do was sew the ball gowns and finagle the teeny tiny cufflinks for the presidents into place. I'd painted the First Lady faces. The bodies were attached and each of the dolls stood on a stand. No rouge for Dolley. As a Quaker, she didn't use any facial enhancements.

The back door opened, and I heard, "I'm back."

Aaron entered the room and gave me a kiss. "Sorry, honey. I'd forgotten about court."

"No problem."

"I'll pick up where I left off with the houses. I'm soon done, thank heavens."

I took out my phone and began snapping picture after picture of every detail in each house, before taking several of the entire house. After photographing the houses, I did the same with the dolls. When taking the photo of Mr. Madison's clothes, I zoomed in to capture the cufflinks, shirt, leggings, and his boots—everything the president wore. Tomorrow, I'd do the same with Dolley's clothes, once they were sewn.

I planned to get a good night's sleep and return early to sew the dresses and clothe the dolls.

"I'll be done after I straighten these pictures." I massaged my sore back. "Why are they always off kilter? It must be from the traffic." My shoulders ached, and my tired eyes barely focused. I removed the first two First Lady pictures, Abigail and Dolley. "Mrs. Adams, I'm glad that you returned to Washington, but did you have to hang the clothes indoors like that? They didn't dry, did they?" I turned to Mrs. Madison. "You sure received a number of recipes today in the mail. Which do you plan to make first? The clam chowder?" I pounded the nails in deeper before they were rehung. "Please have a quiet night. I'm tired of fixing the pictures." I set the hammer on the counter and shifted the other three. I looked over toward Aaron. "I think they're fine now." My stomach began growling as I went over to the front door and double checked the lock.

"I vote for pizza and beer." I shut off the CD player. "Good night, ladies."

"Goofball." Aaron cocked his head. "Perfect." He stood and stretched out his arms, grimacing. "Let's go before I can't move."

"Best words I've heard all day." I walked over to him and we embraced. "Thank you, hon. I couldn't have done it without you."

When I went to lock the back door, the keys weren't where they normally were. I found them at the counter. *Guess I'm too tired to remember where I left them earlier.* We braved the cold and walked a block down to the pizza joint, where we sat and enjoyed the warm atmosphere at a table beside the cozy fireplace.

In the summer, walkers and bikers loved the area because of the towering elm and oak trees that lined the boulevard all the way to the Stone Arch Bridge, which crossed the Mississippi near downtown Minneapolis. The bridge overlooked the tumbling St. Anthony Falls near the historic spot where the Pillsbury and Gold Medal flour mills once stood, dubbing Minneapolis the Flour City. James J. Hill commissioned the bridge to be built in 1883 for his Great Northern Railway.

Enjoying the warmth of the fire, I faced the window and absorbed the few rays left of the day. "I'm starved." I sighed. "It's been a very long two days."

"I know. I'm exhausted." He yawned. "Let's get married over the holidays. What do you say?"

"That's coming up very soon. Let's discuss it with Grandma. At least they shouldn't be too upset with me moving out since I'll still be next door."

"They'll be happy. We can continue using the whirlpool and eating your grandma's delicious cooking. August can keep a close watch on you." He smiled.

"Grandpa enjoys having you around." I took a deep breath and the last two days left my shoulders. "Christmas and the house filled with sparkling lights, just like the stars, and plenty of poinsettias and roses."

Closing my eyes, I reveled in how wonderful it was to be with him. Bing Crosby's voice echoed through my head as I hummed, "*White Christmas.*"

# Chapter Three

Low hanging clouds promised a day of snowfall. Even though it was still early, I might as well get my day started. When I left for work, the brisk, cold air would wake me—that and a huge cup of coffee. I couldn't stop thinking about the upcoming sale of my dollhouses to Jackie Newell and her weirdness about the 'secret' and taking the dolls. My usual drive thru coffee shop wasn't open yet, so I planned to go next door after opening the store.

When I turned into the alley, I noticed Ronnie was parked off to the side, and figured he was waiting for Jackie so he could take more pictures. *How would he know about Jackie?* I locked the door behind me, hung my jacket and dropped my bag inside the workroom before heading into the showroom. Shivers of fear raced up and down my spine the farther I progressed into the room. Something wasn't right. I flipped on the lights.

"Hello," I whispered, hoping it wasn't the ski mask gorilla guy. I glanced behind me. Nothing. While tiptoeing a little further inward, the air seemed to grow cold. "Ladies, are you shivering?" *I am.*

My gaze stopped on the new houses in the showroom that were supposed to be white. Lines of red dribbled from the miniature windows. Curious, I walked closer. My breath caught in my throat and I had trouble breathing as I stared at all the windows. My heart raced as I inched closer. A metallic stench filled my nostrils. I gasped in horror as I got closer. I saw shoes, pants, a body sprawled and a head face first in the Madison house roof. I peered closer and knew it was Jackie Newell because of her hair color.

"Oh my God! Jackie!" It clicked that she might still be alive. Quickly, I felt for a pulse, but knew I wouldn't find any because her body was so still. Her head was positioned in Dolley's boudoir.

The collapsed dollhouse walls and its furnishings had absorbed the blood. The back of Jackie's head was split, but her long hair seemed to have soaked up a great deal of the blood. Blood trickled down the house and onto the table where it followed a line to the floor. My footprints marked where I'd walked through it.

I tried to scream but couldn't find my voice. My heart pounded, as I reached for the phone and called 911.

"Th-th-there's b-b-been a m-murder." I gulped. "Main Street. Northeast. First Lady White House Dollhouse store. Hurry."

"We're sending someone right now."

Within minutes, my store swarmed with men in blue. After being initially questioned about the basic facts, the uniformed officer brought me out to a squad car, where I tried to stare into my store but the number of spectators prevented it. Tears filled my eyes. I admired Jackie because she used her grit and charm to build that wonderful department store. Why would someone want to kill her? Why my shop? My mind was numb and when my phone rang, I couldn't bring myself to answer the call. I glanced at the caller ID. It was from Grandma.

A policeman fetched me as the body was carted away.

"Ms. Anderson?"

"Yes. Liv."

"Please come out to the showroom. The detectives want a minute with you," the officer requested.

"Yes, sir." I followed right behind, staying as close to him as possible. I tried to not look at the house as I passed by, but it was impossible. I shivered, and began shaking at the sight of the body plus the blood.

"Just a minute," Mergens said. He conferred with his partner for a few minutes. "You may leave for now. Go home. Do you have someplace else to stay if you're worried about being alone? We'll be in touch."

"You'll lock up?"

"We'll be here a long time." Mergens frowned. "A very long time. Go home. We know where to reach you."

"Thanks." I was out of the store as fast as lightning.

During the drive home, my mind went in circles as I tried to figure out who would murder Jackie. Why her? I almost drove through a stop sign, and had to tell myself to slow down and focus. I was lucky to have stopped in time, I knew, as I continued onward. At last turning to drive past Howe school, I knew I'd soon be parking and I could finally relax.

When I got home, I found both grandparents sitting in the office waiting for me. Grandma made me a cup of hot chocolate, and I curled up on the settee. It didn't take long before they coaxed the entire story from me. I kept my eyes glued on my phone, hoping for a message from Aaron. Suddenly the back door opened, and we heard, "I'm here, Liv."

"In here!" I jumped up and raced to him, and we clung to each other. We stayed in the kitchen so that we'd be alone.

"You've had quite a shock." Aaron kissed me. "The detectives will want you to return later."

"I figured as much. I know I can handle it alone, but it'd be nice if you drove me."

"We'll wait and see what takes place." He held me close for a moment. "How are you taking it?"

"It was awful. The scene reminded me of the car accident that killed Mommy and Daddy." I burst into tears. "Seeing her dead brought back such memories of seeing my parents die. I should've been dead that day too, if not for my seat belt. But head on! Mommy and Daddy didn't stand a chance. And, now this! Oh God!" I cried into his chest.

"Let it out, baby." Aaron held me tight.

When I looked into his sad eyes, it made me feel sadder.

"Feel any better? It's almost four, and we have a lot to discuss."

"Now that you're here and it's off my chest." Aaron put out his hand and we walked to the office.

"Brave girl we've got here," Aaron said, squeezing my hand. I sat in my former place beside Grandma. "I'm going after another chair." He left, returning right away. "I'll order pizza. How does that sound? Then we're going to have a discussion and try to get to the bottom of what's going on."

"Now? I want to try and forget the whole thing ever happened. However," I waited a beat before continuing, "we need to talk about a few things."

"I'm sure, but let's order something to eat first. Is that all right?" When Grandma and Grandpa nodded, Aaron picked up the phone and ordered a pizza for delivery.

"There has to be some reason for the murder." My brain was starting to come back to life. "The question is, how did she get into the store? What was she after?"

"Let's all do what we need to do, and then reconvene? I need the bathroom," Grandma said. "How about coffee or a soda?"

"Soda." I stood. "I'm showering first and putting on fresh clothes. I still smell the blood on me from when I first found her."

"I'll get them," Aaron said.

I quickly showered, then slipped into a pair of jeans along with a long-sleeved T-shirt with a picture of the 1963 White House Christmas tree on it. I brushed my teeth and pulled my hair into a ponytail. Red ringlets stuck out like springs from the back of my head. I went downstairs and curled up again on the settee. Aaron had set sodas on the small coffee table. He was at the desk with the computer humming. Grandpa was on his chair, smoking a cigar.

"Does this murder have anything to do with the assault?" I took a sip, and the bubbly fizz tickled my nose. I already felt refreshed. "They have to be connected." I took a deep breath, and said, "Did you check out the ten names?"

"Yes, I had a chance to ask around. Your suspects are either living in another state, jail, or aren't physically capable of the crime."

"Thank you," I said. "Do you think the assault and murder are connected?"

"Don't know. Very possible," Aaron responded.

"I wonder what the detectives are thinking?" My brow rose with puzzlement as I glanced at Grandpa.

"Hard to say," Grandpa said.

"They'll have a million more questions. What about cleanup?" Grandma asked.

"Forensics will be calling eventually, then you'll have to go down to the station. They'll take your fingerprints." Aaron looked grimly at me. "Everyone is a suspect, at least until they verify alibis."

"I'd think the bodyguard and secretary would be high on the list." Just then my cell phone buzzed. "It's Max, wondering how I am." I text back, *I'm fine.*

"The pizza will be here any minute." Aaron nodded to the extra chair across from the settee.

"I'm hungry. I'm glad you've ordered one," Grandma said, nodding her head. "I couldn't think after hearing about this. I worried so much about our little Olivia." She patted my hand. "But, I see she's tough and strong, like her mommy."

"Thank you, Grandma." I sighed. "Max had wanted to tell me something, but I hadn't wanted to listen. I was too worried about Jackie coming from New York for possible purchases of dollhouses." I set the soda down. "I'm going to ask. Just a minute." I texted him, asking what he'd meant about wanting to tell me something, and sent the message.

"What was the murder weapon?" Grandpa asked.

"The only thing that comes to mind is the hammer that I keep for fixing things." I started pacing. "It'd have to have been that. What else? The way her head was bashed. Blood was on the floor. Her hair soaked up most of it." I dropped back into the settee. "What an awful way to die. Poor Jackie."

"Now what?" Grandpa asked. "Aaron, you're not holding back, are you?"

"Not at all." Aaron shook his head. "Now we're going to make a list of what we know and don't know."

The doorbell rang, and Aaron went for the pizza.

"My stomach is in knots. I feel so bad for Jackie," I said.

I couldn't eat. As Aaron ate, he typed in everything we knew. I told him about my entering the store, turning on the lights, hanging my coat and throwing my bag in the usual place, then going into the showroom. I told him about the eerie feeling I had when I entered. Talking about seeing the bloody head on the house and calling the police, made me extremely anxious. I remembered little else except all the blood and being petrified. I checked my phone and saw Maggie had left three texts and a voice mail. I sent her a return: *im ok cal latr*.

"Where was the hammer?" Aaron asked.

"I don't remember seeing it." My phone chirruped. Max had texted me back.

*The overhead security camera was knocked out both nights.*

My eyes opened wide. "The killer must've done that."

"What?"

"Max just texted that the overhead security camera was knocked out both nights."

"I'll call right now to report it to the security company, Minnesota Nice," Grandpa said.

"The bodyguard had said, 'Problem solved.' Not sure, but it could mean that he'd put the lights out somehow, such as now they don't need to worry about a video taping during a break-in. They also may have a key," I said. "I'm very worried about this. We need a better alarm system."

"Yes, August, place the call, will you?" Aaron wrote down the number to the security company and handed it to him. "I'm calling the company and letting them know about the security camera." He placed his call and when finished, said, "That helps the investigation."

"Maybe Ronnie has some telltale photos?"

"You never know," Aaron said.

"He also knew about Jackie."

"Jackie was definitely searching for something, otherwise she wouldn't have been there so early," Grandpa stated. "Where's that phone?" Aaron handed it to him.

I waited to answer until he'd finished recording his message to the security company. "She did take those two dolls, but it makes me wonder if they aren't in her purse? Her purse wasn't around. Where was it? I did get the credit card number, but I want the dolls back. They're my creation. I'm curious if there wasn't something special imprinted on them?"

"The police report didn't say anything about missing dolls," Aaron stated, making a separate note to himself.

"She talked about being a descendant, plus something about Mr. Madison's attire."

"Make sure you tell the detectives about all of this." He typed it in. "It'll help in the investigation."

"I'll inform them when I go for fingerprinting." Having my family surrounding me made me feel better, but I was getting frustrated by all the questions. "The bodyguard makes me wary. Why would she need one when she wasn't that big of a celebrity?" I ran my fingers through my hair.

"People have bodyguards for any number of reasons. Stalking, is one," Aaron said. "Ex-husbands, another."

"That's about it. We arranged for Jackie to come at ten and probably purchase the two dollhouses, which you guys know about." Suddenly I started to feel hunger pangs and reached for the remaining slice of pizza.

"What did she say?" Aaron stared at me. "Didn't she ask something weird-like?"

"Oh, yeah, right!" I raised my brow. "She asked if I knew anything about a Madison family secret. I said that I didn't know what she was talking about."

"Family secret?" Grandma sat up straighter. "Madison?"

"Yes, and something about cufflinks. Don't understand any of it." I shook my head.

"It was like she was on a fishing trip," Aaron said, scratching his head.

"Wanda was her secretary and I don't know the bodyguard's name," I said. "I wonder if they've left town?"

"They're probably still in the hotel," Aaron said. "They wouldn't be allowed to leave town yet. All suspects have to be cleared."

"There's one other thing. There's that staircase hidden in the floor behind the counter. Remember? The trapdoor," I asked. "I'll have to point it out to the investigating detectives."

"Wait a minute. Hold that thought, I'm placing a call to the detectives," Aaron said. He made an immediate call and left the room. After a short while, he returned and said, "Detective Erlandsen will be right over."

"While we wait," I said, "Grandma, tell me about the cufflinks. They're the set that once belonged to James Madison, correct? I know that you're holding something back, what is it?"

"Yes, I believe that they are. Someone tried to steal them right after we married, before I inherited them," Grandpa said. "He's dead."

"How do you know?" I asked. "Are they the cufflinks worn at your anniversary and my parents' wedding? I just thought they were from your wedding. That's why they're old."

"Was he incarcerated?" Aaron asked.

"The police informed us. He was sentenced to prison, where he died."

"They're quite valuable, aren't they?"

"Oh yes, very much," Grandma said.

"Where are they?"

"Hidden in a secret place," Grandma said.

"Won't you tell me?"

"Nope," Grandpa said. "It's best for you to not know. They're safe, and that was seventy years ago. This can't be someone looking for these particular cufflinks, there's too much of a time span from that incident to today."

"Jackie mentioned cufflinks, Grandpa. This is too coincidental."

Just then we heard car doors, and saw the detective walk toward the house.

"I'll open the door," Aaron said, getting up. Once the door closed, he said, "Detective Erlandsen, this way." Aaron introduced my grandparents and myself.

"Let's begin. I need to know about the trapdoor," Detective Erlandsen said, looking at Grandpa. "Sir? Mind filling me in?"

"When I bought the building," Grandpa said, "the bottom entrance was closed off. The outside back door is locked. The basement runs through all three buildings. I think it was set up that way for an easy drop and delivery during Prohibition."

"I never thought of that secret exit." I yawned.

"You own the building?"

"No, not anymore. Liv purchased the building."

"Anything else that you've forgotten to tell us, Ms. Anderson?"

"Yes. Jackie removed two dolls before she left that day. I do have her credit card number, but I want them back. They're my creation."

"Dolls?"

"The President and Mrs. Madison miniature dolls."

"Like how big?" He held two fingers apart and asked, "Four inches?"

"Yes. Jackie also asked about Mr. Madison's clothing and his cufflinks, which didn't make any sense. Nor that she asked about a family secret, which I can't explain."

"Okay. Anything else?"

"Yes, I also had trouble finding my keys the other day."

"Duly noted." Detective Erlandsen jotted the information down. "Anything else, call. Here's my card." He handed each one before looking at Aaron, and said, "Keep us up to date if there's anything else that you should think of."

"Will do."

"I'll find my way out."

As soon as he left, I drew in a deep breath. "What a mess to contend with."

"What should I do?" Grandma looked at me.

"You can supervise the cleanup." I frowned. "There's plenty to do."

"Back to security," Grandpa said. "Get the best system there is, installed. We sure don't want this happening again."

"Aaron." Grandpa turned and said, "Now will ya Google that woman? The more we know about a person, the better it'll be."

"I'm right on it." Aaron turned back to the computer and typed in Jackie Newell's name. As he clicked into the different websites, he relayed the information. "There's nothing more that we don't know except for her private plane. She's rich. A major stockholder in the stores. Her family's from the Virginia area. Wait a second here…" He scrolled down and read further, then turned to stare at me. "You're not going to believe this."

"I already know. She's a descendant of Dolley Madison." I smiled. "Which leads to the unanswered question."

"What's the family secret?" Aaron asked.

"Not only that. How do the cufflinks factor into the murder?" I wanted to know.

# Chapter Four

"Is she a descendant of Mr. Madison through a sibling, or from one of Dolley's sisters? I don't have a clue." I rubbed my chin and ran my fingers through my hair. "I'm tired. The question here is; what did she mean by the 'family secret'? She asked twice if I'd heard of it. How can there be one after all of these years? Grandma, do you know what it's about?"

Grandma glanced at Grandpa, and finally said, "No, dear, I've never heard of a family secret. I have an elderly unwed relative who never spoke of a secret."

"Then it's a mystery." I raised my arms in despair. "That's why she was so interested in the Madisons and took those two dolls. Why didn't she just ask me a few questions about them or how long I'd known we were descendants? It sounds like she recently discovered her lineage."

"I'm curious why she wanted the dolls," Aaron stated. "That makes no sense, especially since she planned to purchase the house, dolls plus the furnishings."

"Yes, however, was she really planning to return to purchase the houses?" I asked, puzzled. "It's smart that I took the credit card info or may never be paid."

"I concur with Aaron. Why?" Grandma said.

"There's that unanswered question. She was looking for something and thought she'd found it in the dolls, I bet." I thought about the dolls, but was still perplexed. "I'm going to have to look closely at the clothing to see if there's something that isn't right about them." I shrugged. "What else could it be?"

"I agree with my granddaughter. Why else take them?" Grandpa nodded.

"She should've started talking about being a descendant when we first made contact."

"That gives me an idea." Aaron glanced at Grandpa. "I wonder—no. She wouldn't be short of money, stocks dropping or anything like that, would she?"

"No. I think she had some kind of hair-brained idea."

"It has to do with a 'secret'," I said.

"Very possible," Grandma said.

"Good reasoning." Aaron went back to the website, and clicked out of it.

"I think she wanted money," Grandpa said.

"The root of all evil." Grandma embraced me. "We'll get to the bottom of this. Just you wait and see."

"I hope so, because nothing makes any sense." I thought of a previous message from Montpelier. Since I'm a descendant, they send group e-mails whenever something of interest happens. "There's also been a robbery lately at Montpelier. One of her ruby jewels plus a brooch was taken. There also had been a set of cufflinks that had matched the brooch, but they've been missing for many years."

"Really? Rubies? Brooch? Cufflinks never recovered?" Grandma said, thoughtfully.

"They certainly couldn't be my cufflinks. I wasn't born in the 1700s or 1800s nor stole them," Grandpa said, rubbing his chin. "Talk about a mess."

"Interesting, isn't it?" *I was starting to believe that my dollhouses weren't the only reason Jackie of New York! had quickly become a customer. My dreams of the big time, were now at the bottom of the pit.* I noticed a glint in Grandma's eye, like she was hiding something such as the whereabouts of Dolley's keepsakes. *I'll have to question her later.* "A break-in at the Madison Estate."

"Cufflinks and rubies." Aaron massaged his chin. "She must've known about the theft. I wonder if this isn't the 'secret' she spoke about? Maybe this is why she came here?" He looked at me. "I wonder if the Montpelier thief is a descendant?"

"But, the cufflinks weren't stolen recently. See? Nothing is right," I said, yawning. "If they've been in your family for hundreds of years, then the missing cufflinks could be yours." I looked at Grandpa.

"We're jumping to conclusions here, guys." Grandpa took a deep breath. "One thing at a time."

"You're right, Grandpa." I mulled it over in my mind. "Read the entire article, Aaron, so they can hear about it."

"I wish you'd told us about it right away, Liv," Grandpa said.

"There isn't much else to say." Aaron scratched his chin. "Here goes: The Montpelier estate, home to James and Dolley Madison, was broken into recently. The thieves stole a set of rubies and a brooch purported to have once belonged to Mrs. Madison and given to her by her husband, the President. Mr. Madison had a set of matching cufflinks, but Mrs. Madison bequeathed them to a dear friend, Elijah Putnam, upon her death. They have never been located. The hope is that someday, the person who'd inherited them would eventually donate them to the museum."

"See what I mean? It can't be my cufflinks. They weren't stolen. They're safely hidden away and haven't been seen by me for many years," Grandpa declared. "They're right here in the desk under this rose." He indicated the spot. "Press down it'll pop open."

"Do it, August," Grandma said.

"Another time, we're all tired," Grandpa said.

"I'm going to look later, Grandpa," I said. "I am tired so you're right."

"Any idea who this Elijah Putnam is?" Grandma asked. "That's a very old sounding name, isn't it?"

"Is there a picture of the jewelry?" I wondered if the images would match the cufflinks and the gems that my dolls wore. "Grandma? You look deep in thought. What is it?"

"Nothing, dear. Nothing at all. I'm just thinking about Dolley and why she'd give away the cufflinks, that's all. She was very poor upon her death."

"The cufflinks were passed down to me through the ages, and I have a letter to prove it. I'm not sure if there's a Putnam in my family tree. If there is, then they need to be donated to the museum," Grandpa said.

"You're right. We'll have to research that name," I said, thinking it through. "What a quandary."

"Your father wore them for your parents' wedding, and our sixtieth anniversary photo. Aaron can wear them. By the time of your wedding, we'll know if they should be donated."

"Okay, but I plan to look at them soon. They need to be put in the bank deposit box. They shouldn't be here, that's for sure." I sipped from my drink. "I want to look at the pictures of the stolen brooch and jewelry again."

"Come here and take a look." Aaron got up from the chair, and walked around to the side of the desk.

"Aren't they beautiful?" I sat down. "The images of the brooch and gems are clear." I stared at the monitor. The large dropped ruby gem with the smaller gems strung with tiny starred diamond necklace looked gorgeous and fit for a queen. The rubies, sapphires, and diamonds on the brooch, patterned a flag of the United States as it would've looked at the time, and similarly like the cufflinks. A gadroon encircled it, but the article didn't say what the imprint read. A shiver raced up and down my spine as I further read the enlarged card next to the empty cufflink stand. "Given to Elijah Putnam, 1849."

"What do you make of it, honey?" Aaron peered over my shoulder.

"That is her death date—1849. The picture of the cufflinks isn't very clear, but there's something familiar about it." My brows narrowed as I got up closer to the picture. "I just can't put it together." I waited a minute and asked Grandpa, "Do the cufflinks you own have a gadroon imprint?"

"Yes, but I don't remember what's in it. It's been so many years and because of the thwarted burglary, I haven't really looked at them since our wedding. I'd like to know for sure about the ancestry. Did you know that my ancestors came from Virginia?" Grandpa asked.

"No. But, a lot of Scotsmen settled in that area. It's not unusual." I continued studying the image. "Interesting, though." I got up and started walking over to the settee to rest beside Grandma. "I wish they'd call for me. I want to go to bed." No sooner had I made the remark than the phone rang.

Aaron was logging out of the computer and shutting it down just then, and said, "You should get it."

"Right." I picked it up and the group listened to my one-sided conversation.

"The forensic team needs me to come down to walk them through the crime scene."

"I'll take her," Aaron answered. "She'll need a ride home, and I want to find out what's happening."

"Look after her," Grandpa said.

"He will." I turned to Aaron. I walked around the desk.

"You're right." Aaron set his soda down. "Good night."

"I'll be home as soon as possible." I kissed Grandma and Grandpa on the cheek. "Don't worry about me."

We grabbed our coats and walked, arm in arm, to Aaron's van out back. I was glad that Aaron would drive, since I clearly wasn't in the mood. As we climbed into the van, my mind was elsewhere.

"What are you thinking about?" Aaron drove swiftly through downtown. Thankfully, there was little traffic this time of night.

"Jackie, my mom and dad, grandma, me. How does this all tie together?" I glanced at him. "We're missing an important piece of the puzzle. Did Jackie die because she thought we had the cufflinks? That's how I see it. Did she think that the dolls held the key? Are the cufflinks on the Mr. Madison dolls, the same as the stolen cufflinks?"

I thought a moment. "The company that makes the men's clothing allows me to order the outfits for specific presidents. The new shipment of clothes has Madison's slightly different because the cufflinks are already drawn into the shirt sleeve cuff."

"Painted on? That's what she saw and wanted a closer look. The cufflinks." We turned onto Washington Avenue and drove across the bridge, then down Main Street and parked in the back.

"I saw the light on out front."

"Hmm. Max's truck isn't here. He must be out for the night."

"I'm not thinking about that right now." I climbed out of the car and went to the back door, where we were greeted by a police officer.

"The detectives are inside," the officer said.

"We ask you both to refrain from touching anything. We just want you, Liv, to tell us the path you took this morning when you entered the building—beginning with what you touched. Then we'll take it from there, and you'll be free to go."

"Try not to personalize it. Maybe it'll be easier," Aaron encouraged me.

"I'll try."

Aaron stayed behind as I followed the detective into the showroom. My heart pounded. My mind flashed back to the head, face down in my dollhouse. "What a miserable death. I feel so bad for her. No one deserves to die like that. No one." I took a deep breath. "It still smells of blood."

"Yes ma'am." Detective Erlandsen glanced over to us. "Just take your time. We'll be here all night, so there's no need to rush."

"Okay. Give me a minute." I blew my nose and wiped my eyes. I knew that I could go through with the exercise. I took a deep breath before starting, "I entered the back way with a key, then flicked on the hall light before going into the workroom. I hung my coat and bag on the clothes tree. At least I think I did. I know I went into the workroom and turned on the light."

"So far, two light switches." He made a notation in his pad. "Touch anything else back there?"

"No." I shook my head. "I had an eerie feeling. It was six o'clock and Jackie Newell was expected at ten. There still was plenty to do to get her dollhouses ready." I looked at Aaron, who gave me an assuring nod. "Then I walked into the showroom and turned on the lights. That's when I noticed the feet, legs, head, face down in the Madison house."

"Where did you walk?"

"My footprints are still in the blood, by the table. You can see them." I looked at the floor, now covered with a plastic tarp. My insides curdled. I clutched my stomach. "Just a minute." Covering my mouth, I raced to the restroom and barfed. I moved to the sink and doused my face, then grabbed a paper cup to rinse my mouth. My cheeks were flushed when I returned to the showroom. "Sorry."

"It happens to the best of us." Detective Mergens shrugged.

I felt like an imbecile. I figured he probably wrote down that I chucked it all up, since he was making notations of everything I said or did.

"Continue." Detective Erlandsen peered closely at the ruined dollhouse.

"That's it. I reached for the phone—this one." I pointed to it. I continued with my spiel of what I'd touched or what happened. "Done?"

"Yes. We'll call you in the morning." Detective Erlandsen glanced through his notes.

"Good night," Detective Mergens stated.

"You too," I said.

We took that to mean that we were dismissed. I yawned all the way home.

"You're staying with me, aren't you?" Aaron asked, parking in the garage.

"Of course." With his arm across my back, we walked into the house.

I sat for quite a long while and wrote on my laptop to Maggie, to keep her up to date of the events.

It was midnight when we fell into bed.

I must've been exhausted, because I slept like a rock. I woke to Aaron frying bacon, and hurried to meet him. "Morning." I kissed him. "Should I put down the toast?"

"Nope. I can handle it. I've got some good news."

"What's that?"

"Two suspects were questioned."

"I bet it's Wanda Brown or the bodyguard, Stone Rogers."

"Probably, but I'm not part of the investigation." He dished up the bacon and I buttered the toast. "I just hear little tidbits."

"They'll be behind bars soon, I hope." We ate, and I said, "I'd better get home and shower, then get to work. What a mess ahead of me. I wonder if they'll be done?"

"Should be. High profile like that? They'll work through the night."

I cleaned up the kitchen, and we promised to meet up later. I hiked across the backyard, and let myself into the house.

Grandma and Grandpa had already left for their early morning breakfast with some old grade school pals. Grandma had left two notes for me where she knew I'd see them. I believed she was a schoolteacher at heart and truly missed her calling when she married Grandpa. Almost every note she wrote was either multiple choice, true or false, or an essay. She'd cleverly line up the notes with answer choices. A letter was always printed in front of each choice such as a T or F for me to circle, or leave room for a short reply. Today's note was multiple choice. It read:

*A) Don't want to see Grandpa's family Bible:*

*B) Want to:*

*C) Want to but not until the murder gets cleared up: or*

*D) Drop the subject entirely.*

I chose B, since I figured it would keep my mind off the situation and I might find it interesting.

The second note was a simple true or false question.

*Will you be in the store this morning around ten o'clock to let the cleaning ladies come?*

*T or F.*

I circled T.

I glanced out to the back window at Aaron's house. His car wasn't parked in the driveway. I hoped he'd be able to give me an update about the case when he returned home.

After my morning routine, I climbed into my car and headed toward the store. My anxiety ratcheted up a few notches as I parked. Several unknown cars occupied the parking spaces behind the building. When I stepped from the car, cameras clicked as Ronnie took one picture after another.

"Shoo! Go away!" I hollered as I marched up to the door. I glared at all the reporters and shouted, "Shame on you!"

"Just trying to make a livin'!"

"One was enough!" I shut my mouth and prayed that a video wouldn't end up on Facebook or YouTube.

With shaky fingers, I unlocked the door and stepped inside, quickly locking it behind me. Quietly I walked in further, turning on the workroom lights. Everything seemed normal. The painted dolls still stood on the stands.

"Good morning, sweethearts. I hope you're not too cold, honeybees. I'll dress you as soon as possible."

The fabric lay across the sewing machine ready for sewing. The boxes with the unsorted items were still stacked against the wall where we had left them. The workbench was also clean. I didn't see blood on the floor. I was relieved.

"My poor girls," I said. I stood inside the showroom, studying the mess. The historical houses were junk, of course. I glanced at Mrs. Lincoln, she had tears in her eyes. "Mrs. Lincoln, it'll be fine. The cops will get the killer." I walked to Mrs. Kennedy. "There, there now. You're brave." I ended by Mrs. Ford. "Shall we all dance on top of the table, just like you did on the presidential desk? It'll liven everyone up."

I frowned as I walked to the computer. I noticed more blood on the second newly built dollhouse. I didn't notice that last night, probably because they were small specks. I went to the computer and started it. As it booted up, I gave Mikal a call to ask if he'd mind shooing away the press and go for coffee with me. He said he'd be delighted to stomp on them. I grabbed my bag, locked the door then tentatively stepped out.

"Hurry, Livvie." Mikal placed his arm over my shoulder, blocking photographers from taking our picture as we hurried down to the coffee shop.

"How's it going?" Mikal peered down at me once we were safely inside. "You look worn out. Not your cheery self. Sounds like the last few days have been stressful, with the break-ins and all." He ordered his favorite—a Greek coffee—and an Irish cream latté for me.

"I'm tired and feel like I've been run over by a semi. Actually I'm full of anxiety and fear, but trying not to think about it." I shivered. "There's blood on the floor of my shop. Two of my dollhouses are ruined because of some splatters of blood. I had to come over last night to show the forensic team what and where I'd touched or stepped. Grandma's lining up cleaning ladies."

"Can Max still stay in his apartment?"

"Of course. He'll speak to security when they arrive. We all have our projects. Out of my own curiosity, I'm going to do more research on Jackie Newell, plus I still have a lot of sorting to do from the first break-in." I sipped my coffee.

"Keep washing your hands and pretend you're washing your face, and brush yourself off all day long. That should help to rid all the bad karma surrounding you."

"Never thought of that." The man amazed me. He always came up with these weird ideas, but when he'd relay them, they make sense. If I told someone else to pretend to wash themselves, they'd most likely set me up with a psychiatrist. "I probably do have an awful colored aura." I shuddered. "Finding someone dead definitely will stop you short. I never want that to happen again." I held my coffee cup tight.

"You're strong. You'll manage. I have just the thing that'll cheer you up. I bought two DVDs of Mitch Miller and his sing along television show." Mikal sipped his coffee and glanced out. "Oh, good Lord. The vulture is still waiting for us. I'm surprised he didn't follow us inside." He took a deep breath. "Are you ready? We'll go into my place, and I'll give you the DVD and a reading."

"Thanks. I could use one."

We dashed outside, still clinging to our coffees and rolls. Mikal stepped aside as we reached his store, letting me go inside first after he unlocked it.

"Finally. When will they go away?" We locked the door and made sure the front shades covered the windows.

"Probably not for a few days, sweetie. Sorry." He sat in his chair and crossed his arms. "What a nightmare." He giggled. "It is kind of funny but horrid at the same time, isn't it?" Mikal shook his head. "You'd think Ronnie would move onto more news, like fish stolen from Lake Nokomis. Even in death, the woman needs privacy."

"You do have a point. People are rude."

"Second thought, let's do a handwriting analysis. That'll tell us more about the present situation." He reached for a tablet and pen, and slid it over to me. "Write five lines. It can be anything—even nonsense, but not the same thing over and over."

He went for the DVD then sat back down and sipped his coffee as I wrote: *Max is worried and so is Aaron. Grandma is a sweetheart. Jackie was a distant relative of Dolley's and thought there is some sort of a family secret and it's connected to Mr. Madison's cufflinks. I think this is what got her deader than a doornail. I have no idea what the secret's about. Why would Grandma want me to look through Grandpa's family Bible? Maybe he's related to Dolley too. Wouldn't that be a stitch? Both grandparents related to Dolley? That would make them distant cousins. Kissing cousins. Eeew! Don't want to go there! Where are my two Madison dolls?*

"Here." I slid the tablet back to him. "Now you can see that my mind is going around in circles." I slipped the DVD into my bag. "Thanks."

"Circles. Swimming is more like it. But that's okay, because writing it out helps you to clarify and put order into your thinking." Mikal took out his large magnifying glass and studied the handwriting. "You haven't lost your sense of humor through this ordeal, which is good. I believe that's what will keep you going—that and your fine wit. You'd better be careful." He frowned and looked at me over his glasses. "You must not go into small rooms. Stay away from them." His brow knit together like a brush as he further studied my writing. "You'll do fine as long as you remember that."

"Small rooms?" I finished my coffee, and neither of us said anything for a few minutes. "That's settled. I won't hide under a bed."

"I believe it's referring to your quest for the dolls. Under the bed is a small place and so are closets." He offered me the paper, but I waved it away.

"What are you saying?" I stood and dropped my empty cup in the garbage.

"If you plan to pursue the dolls, find another way to go about it. Don't sneak around. Your red hair and freckles are memorable."

"I get it. Find a disguise."

"Not that I know what you're planning to do."

"Neither do I." I took a deep breath. "Time to run."

I sneaked out the back way. Ronnie was standing at the corner, and shouted, "What was it like to find a dead person? Why was she in the store? How was she killed?"

The door opened from the inside and Max jerked me in.

"Want me to pop him for ya?" He pulled me close, and kicked the door closed. I saw anger in his eyes and his gentle touch was full of concern. With the latching of the door lock, I felt relief.

"Right in the kisser."

# Chapter Five

I thought it was my heart pounding and beating loudly, but it was someone at the backdoor. "Answer it," I whispered to Max. "Pop the vulture in the mouth." The person knocked harder.

"Listen, Livvie." Max caught my arm. "Everything will work out."

"I hope so. This is one huge nightmare, and one that won't go away for a long time, I fear." I went into the showroom as he opened the door.

"Dolley?" I whispered near the doll. "Don't worry because I won't let any harm come to you." I greeted each of the dolls as I strolled to the front counter.

No sooner had I sat down in front of the computer when Max entered with two men who were dressed in blue shirts and jeans.

"Here's the lady in charge." Max stared at me. "I'm here to supervise."

"Minnesota Nice Security System. We're here to take a look and get you the best system possible for your business." Each man showed his credentials and shook my hand. The logo on their shirts was a Viking ship.

"Minnesota Nice, as in Norwegian?" I smiled and glanced at the older man's business card. "Leif Erickson."

"You betcha!" His eyes twinkled.

"And I'm the other half of the business, Sigurd Oleson."

*Thank heavens, you didn't say Ole,* I chuckled to myself, thinking of all the Ole and Lena jokes that are passed around, especially with all the Scandinavians in this area. "Max can answer just about everything. I trust his judgment." I looked at Max.

"Let's get started by looking the place over."

"Right this way." Max guided them outside.

I finally logged into the store's website and brought up the images of the dolls and dollhouses. They were beautiful and made me smile. It gave me the strength and courage to read through the e-mails from the past few days. Most were sympathetic and hoped that I didn't plan to shut down, or that the culprit wasn't a nutsy stalker. I clicked out of the site and went into the daily newspaper, only to find a picture of Jackie facedown on the dollhouse as the lead story. The photo was submitted by Ronnie. Not wanting to read any more about it, I closed out and went to my personal e-mail account. I opened the link from last night about Dolley Madison.

After rereading the article, I became more confused. It didn't make sense for Dolley to bequeath the cufflinks to someone other than her son. When I'd researched our lineage, it was apparent that Dolley's son, John Payne Todd, was a gambler and always in debt to his stepfather. Mr. Madison continually paid Todd's debts without telling his wife, and this became the reason for the sale of the estate after his death. After the estate sale, Dolley lived in Washington, and her income barely kept her alive. She relied on the goodness of people to give her food, including her former slave who helped save the George Washington portrait from the fire. Since she lived on a pittance, why hadn't she sold the cufflinks and the rest of the jewelry? Maybe she was afraid that her son would gamble them away, and they'd be lost forever? With the saving of the George Washington portrait, it was apparent that she had a sense of future historical value. She'd rather preserve treasures than sell them even if it meant living as a pauper.

I uploaded the pictures from the article and studied them. The cufflinks on my President Madison doll were similar to the image shown in the article. Now I knew why the cufflinks had seemed so familiar. They were almost identical.

Just as I started searching the Putnam name, my phone rang. The cleaning ladies were out back, but the door was locked. I jumped up, and by the time I got to the back door, Max had opened it to let the two women enter with equipment and cleaning supplies.

"Come in. Thanks," I said to Max who went out to the security team. "I'll show you around." I opened the restroom door and turned on the light as they set their stuff down. "That's the only water supply in the store." I then showed them the workroom. "Ask before you start in here. The other room is far more important." We stood at the entrance to the showroom. "Are you ready? There's blood which needs removing from the floor."

"It's okay. We know what to do. I'm Ruth." The woman wore patched jeans plus a gray T-shirt, and her head was topped with a worn scarf. She was stocky with short, stubby fingers.

"I'm Suzy. We'll be fine, don't worry." This woman was short and wiry, pinched face with her hair brought back in a tight bun. A scarf also covered her hair. She carried the largest tin bucket that I'd ever seen.

"This is worse than a few cuts and bruises." When the two just looked at me like I was an idiot, I said, "Follow me and you shall see."

I stood aside and watched as the cleaning ladies gawked and stared at the pool of blood under the table and the smashed dollhouse. "The house has to be removed, of course, and discarded. The blood has to be washed from the floor and table. We may just have to trash that too. You can see that the blood has flowed out across the hardwood floor. All those bumps and ripples that old floors have, you know?" I took a deep breath. "Do what you can. That's all I can hope for." I tried not to laugh. "You can start by removing the house."

"This will keep us busy." Ruth nudged Suzy. "We've done this before, so don't worry." She sighed. "Poor woman."

"Yes, poor woman. Uff da," Suzy said.

"I'll let you two get started." Where on earth had Grandma dug up these old Norwegians from? Had she looked them up in the Runestone Museum in Alexandria, or dug them out from under the Hjemkomst Museum in Moorhead, which contained a replica of the original Viking ship? Or maybe they ate too much pickled herring? "I'll be right here if you need anything."

"Jumpin' jiminy." Suzy glanced at Ruth and said, "Let's get started."

"Are you all set?" I asked, looking at one and then the other.

"Of course." Ruth eyed Suzy. "Let's take care of the house first. We'll round up the disposal bags. The big ones are in the truck."

"You betcha."

"You've done jobs like this before?" I asked, raising a brow. "There can't be much of a market in Minneapolis for blood removal."

"You'd be surprised," Ruth said.

"We can do it," Suzy said.

"You two seem to know what to do." Watching them, I noted how they carefully walked the circumference of the table. "I'll be right here if you need anything." I moved over to the computer and sat down, covering my mouth to stifle my laughter. When they left the room, I let go. It felt so good to laugh that I couldn't stop.

"The cleaning ladies are a stitch-in-a-half," I whispered to Max who just entered.

"They must be. They each had a drink from their very own flask when they thought I wasn't looking."

"Oh my. I'll have to keep a lookout for that."

It didn't take long before the crew returned to remove the house. Both carried the remnants of it outside.

Dorrie was soon to arrive to help me sort through the box of disheveled pieces from the break-in.

I sat once again by the computer and watched as Ruth entered the room wearing heavy gloves, dragging something that reminded me of a vacuum cleaner.

"I think, they're the cleanup crew from a Seven Corners watering hole. They're old enough that they may be able to give you first-hand pointers on the dollhouse furnishings." Max raised his brow and looked down at me.

"They're just what I needed this morning." The Seven Corners section of Minneapolis was located near the West Bank of the Mississippi River where several streets met, making seven corners. In close proximity to the University of Minnesota, the area was notorious for its many bars. "The mayor is trying to clean up the neighborhood. It's called revitalization," I sarcastically said to Max. Then I remembered he needed to ask a question about the security company. "The Minnesota Nice squad?"

"The cleaning ladies do look like they know what they're doing," Max eyes crinkled.

"They amuse me," I said.

"Oh yeah." Max grinned and pulled a sheet of paper from his pocket. "The security guys need a down payment of five hundred. You or Grandpa?"

"Let me see." I grabbed the paper and perused it. "Wow!" I folded it before shoving it into my pocket. "When will they be back?"

"They'll start wiring tomorrow."

"Okay." Just then the bell jingled over the front door. Fortunately it was Dorrie. "Lock it, will ya?"

"Sure." Dorrie's tree-shaped dangling earrings fit with the rest of her dress, green in color with gold wreaths printed on it. "These the cleaning ladies?" Dorrie nodded toward the women, mouthing "them"?

"Yep." I rolled my eyes as I bit back a giggle.

"That stench kinda gets to ya, ya know," Dorrie said. "I'm glad it's almost cleaned." Dorrie brushed her hands together. Looking at me, she asked, "Workroom?"

"If you would, please?" I logged out of the account, and let the computer sleep. She was already setting a box on the workbench when I entered.

"Should I take the dolls up to my apartment for now?" Max leaned against the counter, his arms crossed. "It's probably the safest, so they won't accidentally get broken by Suzy or Ruth." He cocked his head.

I had to steer my gaze off of the women. "Good idea. Do you want Dorrie to help carry them?"

"I'd be more than happy," Dorrie piped up. She held out her arms as he loaded them with small boxes.

I got started sorting as they walked out together. I piled up miniature emerald green velveteen curtains. Red velveteens were to be used in Dolley's drawing room in the White House, the place where she exercised non-partisanship and won the hearts of many politicians. It's now called the Red Room.

I paid no attention to the time as it slipped slowly by, nor did I notice the comings and goings of Max, Dorrie or the cleaning ladies. I turned when I heard my name.

"Want to come and see?" Suzy asked. I noticed her tired eyes as she leaned against the doorframe. "What a nightmare this mess is."

"Sure. I'm coming." I wiped my hands on a towel before following her. "Where's Ruth?"

"She's taking a break."

"Oh, I see."

"Not too bad, eh?" She stood next to the computer counter and watched me as I walked the perimeter and checked out the floor. The table legs still had blood smears near the bottom. "Can't you get the stain out?" I touched the small marks with my shoe.

"No. Pretty tough." She walked to one certain area and tapped the floor. It was the spot where the pool of blood had been the thickest. "Soaked in, here. The floor needs stripping and polishing in order to get it out properly, ma'am."

I knelt down and peered closely at the hardwood planks. She was right. The brown spot was large, and it would show with direct light. It needed professional care.

"You're right. You two did a wonderful job, better than hoped for." I stood up and looked at her. "Thank you." I started for the cash drawer by the computer, and went to open it.

"You'll get billed. We're paid through the cleaning service, so we're good."

"Here's a tip," I said, handing over a fifty-dollar bill. "Split it, will you? Thanks again."

I followed her to the door. I could see through their van window that Ruth's head was rolled back with her jaw hanging down. *Bet she's snoring!* "Take care."

"Will do," Suzy called.

I closed the door with relief and went back into the room and sat down. A headache was starting, but I reached for the phone instead of looking for a pain reliever. I called Grandma.

"Grandma, the cleaning ladies just left." I walked out to the showroom and rolled up the shades. I told her about Ruth and Suzy and how professional they were. "We need someone now to take care of the floor." As we disconnected, I glanced at the clock. It was already two o'clock and I hadn't eaten. No wonder I had a headache. I was thinking about asking Dorrie and Max if they wanted to order some takeout when I looked out the window and saw an unmarked squad car parking. I put the phone into my pocket. "Shoot! So much for lunch."

I watched the two detectives exit from the car and walk up to the store.

Dorrie entered from the backroom and walked over to stand beside me. I was happy to see her as I opened the door for the detectives.

"Dorrie Fillmore, correct?"

"Yes."

"Why don't you and Ms. Fillmore go into the backroom where it's more private?" Detective Erlandsen said to Mergens.

"Oh. Whatever." Dorrie gave me a puzzled look as they walked away.

"I'd like to run through the questioning once more. Maybe something will trigger something useful." Detective Erlandsen cleared his throat and repeated his question about where the body was found.

"Yes, it was right here." We were standing beside the spot.

"You had a break-in two days earlier, my notes tell me. Do you think the two crimes are related?" He arched his brow.

"I don't know," I said. "Isn't that your job to figure out?" I placed my hands on my hips. "Don't you have anyone else to pester? Someone who stood to gain from her death?"

"We're checking alibis at the moment, ma'am."

"I'm sorry, but I'm at my wits end. I was at home in bed sleeping. We'd pulled an all-nighter just to get the dollhouses ready for Jackie. I came back to the store early that morning to put the finishing touches on them as well as sew the dolls' dresses. That's when I found the body. I don't have anything else to say."

"She was killed by a blunt instrument."

"It had to be the hammer which I'd left on the counter the night before."

"So it's not a surprise?"

I shook my head.

"We're waiting for the lab results." Erlandsen looked deeply into my eyes and I gulped. "Tell me about the missing two dolls."

"Jackie Newell took Mr. and Mrs. Madison for some unknown reason when she visited the shop earlier. The dolls are handmade. Everything in my store is. Max carves the heads, I paint them and sew the women's clothing but purchase the men's. They are my creation and should be treated like that. As a matter of fact, I should look into copyrights."

"Valuable dolls."

"They're collector's items."

"Oh, I see." He jotted down a few notes on his pad. "Who was with Ms. Newell when she came into the store the first time?"

"Her secretary, Wanda Brown. Her bodyguard, Stone Rogers, came in a little later." I thought for a moment and remembered something. "It was strange, because he stood right inside the door and said, 'problem solved'."

"What," he raised his brow, "do you suppose was meant by that?"

"Not a clue." The workroom door opened, and Detective Mergens and Dorrie walked toward us. Dorrie's once happy face looked a little anxious.

"I believe we're done, for now." At the front door, they stopped and turned around. "We'll be in touch."

# Chapter Six

When the front door closed behind the detectives, I locked it with a flourish. My cheeks burned, and hot tears streamed down them. I sniffled and blew my nose as I walked over to the computer counter only to slump into the chair. My mind was swimming with what ifs.

*What if I hadn't researched our lineage and found that Grandma and I were related to Dolley Madison?* Then Jackie wouldn't have been murdered.

But, where did all the second-guessing lead me?

What did this all mean? I wondered if I shouldn't try to sneak into the hotel room where Wanda and Stone are staying? I wondered if Jackie saw something different on the doll clothes from what's pictured in photographs? I glanced at the clock, and it was already mid-afternoon.

Dorrie's voice interrupted my thoughts.

I looked at her. "Say what?"

"Can I just leave? I'm exhausted. I feel like a traitor and a horrible person along with the fact that I should just go home and slit my wrists." She stared at me. "But, I do feel horrible for answering questions about you." She was beet red, and I felt sorry for her. "He bugged me. All those questions." She stared ahead for

61

a moment. "He wanted to know how you've acted. Happy, sad… If you've been nervous today. Drop any hints? Said anything weird, like "glad that's done with." That sort of thing." She blew out a long a breath. "It's given me the creeps. Also, I keep thinking about the missing dolls." She looked hard at me. "You were so excited and nervous about Jackie coming here. Why did she want them?"

"Your guess is as good as mine."

"What was Jackie after?"

"I wish I knew, but it might have something to do with the cufflinks on Mr. Madison," I said, wondering why she was so curious. "Hold that thought." I held up a finger before picking up my phone. I gave Aaron a buzz. When he answered, I said, "Hey. Where are you and have you heard anything about Jackie's death?" I hoped he'd tell me something good about the situation, but he had nothing to add. I disconnected and looked back to Dorrie. "Aaron, me, Grandpa and Grandma are going to discuss matters tonight." I frowned. "I really don't have anything else to say."

"What's eating you?" Dorrie asked.

"I'm not sure." I sank deeper in my chair. "I have this niggling feeling that this murder runs deeper than anyone could imagine. You already know that I'm a descendant of Dolley Madison, so was Jackie." I looked at Dorrie, whose mouth was shaped like an 'O,' but she had an odd look in her eye. "And that's not all. There was a break-in at Montpelier a few weeks ago. Also, a few of Dolley's gems were stolen."

"It might all be a coincidence, you know, the cufflinks." Dorrie raised a brow. "What else is on your mind?"

"Dolley had to adhere to the expectations of the day, such as embroidery and other handiwork." My thoughts went to Grandma's First Lady dolls and the embroidered sampler adorning her wall. "I'm willing to bet that the Dolley Madison connection is somehow central to the investigation. Dolley kept many secrets and rumors to herself, you know? She was an amazing woman and First Lady."

"Yes, she was." Dorrie's eyes flashed. "Oh wow! She did embroider your grandmother's sampler, right? Maybe the secret's right in the words on the sampler, and you don't even know it." She studied me. "Ever thought about that?"

"I haven't a clue about what Jackie referred to when she asked me about the family secret, but I'm going to give it some thought as well as the cufflinks." I watched Dorrie closely because I wanted to catch her reaction. Dorrie and I never did hit it off as friends when we were kids. She was jealous of me. Whenever I got something new, she did too. For birthday parties, she'd always invite more people than I. She'd stick her tongue out at me when I'd get a good grade or the teacher would say something nice about me. It seems that we've always been slightly at odds with each other.

"You'll have to inspect the two dolls carefully. The killer might find the missing clue to the family secret before you." Dorrie stared into the distance. "What a week."

"You're right, but how would they know?" I still wondered if I should risk getting the dolls? "And, how would I ever get them?"

"Max? Maybe he could help?"

"No. The police will probably return them." I groaned. "I'm starved."

"Me too." Dorrie grinned. "Fries and a soda?"

"On me." Just as I stood, Max entered from the back.

"What's up? It's dead in here." He stopped, and said, "Oops! Completely tasteless."

"Yes, you are. We're going for a soda, fries, and burgers." Dorrie hiked past him to the workroom with me following. "You coming?"

"Of course." He came up behind me.

"I think we need a break." I looked in my bag to check to make sure that I had everything. The mail had come and I dumped the new Smithsonian magazine into it to read later. "Let's head out. I'm thirsty and hungry and completely sick of everything." I slipped into my winter jacket.

"I'll lock up." Max locked up as we walked out.

Fresh, crisp air brightened my spirits. As we walked down the block to the nearest restaurant, my thoughts went back to the dolls.

No sooner had we sat down at one of the corner tables, than I noticed Ronnie sitting off to the side with other reporters with his camera around his neck.

"Liv?" Ronnie took a quick snapshot. "Heard anything?"

Max jumped up and took his camera. "Invasion of privacy," Max stated. "Now leave."

"I want my camera back." Ronnie glared.

"Nope. No way. Get outta here," Max said.

"You haven't heard the last from me." Ronnie sulked away with his hands in his pockets.

"What was that all about?" I asked. "He's a pain, but why take away his camera?"

"He bugs me," Max stated.

At that moment the waitress came by to take our order. "Put it all on my tab." I ordered a cheeseburger and a lite beer. The other two did the same. When she left, I looked at Max. "He bugs me too. Thanks."

"Glad to."

"Why the picture?" Dorrie asked.

"Who knows? We've both known him for years, so he probably is still mad that I didn't date him."

"That was years ago. He needs to get over it," Dorrie commented.

The waitress came over with the pitcher of soda and glasses, and set them down. She walked away.

"The police never let up, do they?" Max took a sip of his beverage.

"You were questioned too?" Dorrie's eyes opened wider.

"You mean again?" I stared at Max.

"Yes." Max took another sip, as did Dorrie and I.

"I think they're trying to link me to the killing."

"Nah. Just their job." He smiled at me. "It's the order of things."

"Thanks. I needed to hear that." I lifted my glass and took a long swallow.

The waitress carried the cheeseburgers over and set them down. Dorrie smothered her burger in ketchup. I did too. We dug in, and gave each other a smile as we bit into our first bite.

Not surprisingly, Max finished first. Both our cell phones buzzed simultaneously. Our eyes met as we dug our phones out to read the text messages. Mine read:

*6 at your house.*

"See you later." Max got up, scooting his chair back. "I've got an errand to run."

"Thanks for everything today, Max," I said. As he walked away, I realized that another day had nearly passed, and they weren't any closer to discovering the murderer's identity. As I was deep in thought, I didn't hear Dorrie. "What?"

"Is he always this mysterious?" She finished her drink after swallowing her last bite of cheeseburger.

"Yep. He keeps to himself."

"He never said much when I helped him." Her eyes became the size of saucers. "We barely talked. He spent the whole time going on about the store and the murder. I guess it's time for me to tell you, but, I'm married, I'll have you know."

"Really? I didn't know. You said he was a boyfriend?" *Another lie.* "To whom?"

"We'll come over sometime, and have fun. You'll love him. I want to keep our marriage a secret right now for personal reasons. Brad's a student and drove the limo for Jackie. The bodyguard occupied the front seat."

"Oh my gosh. Well, I can't wait to meet him." I waved at the waitress, and handed my debit card to her. After signing the check, I said, "Let's call it a day, and I'll pay you the full day's wages. I'm not sure what tomorrow will bring or when I'll be ready to open again. How about if I give you a call? Does that sound okay? Sorry about all of this." I stood.

"That's fine. None of this is your fault. I'll be waiting." She stood, and gave me a hug before walking away.

As I watched her leave, I felt bad about of the murder because of how it had thrust everyone I cared about right into the middle of the investigation. I picked up my bag and walked back to where my Focus was parked. I decided to give Erlandsen a call to inquire about my dolls. His answer was a terse, "Detective Erlandsen speaking."

"Liv Anderson, here. I'm curious to know if you've recovered my dolls?"

"Not yet, ma'am. The person in question claims that she doesn't have them."

"The little thief. She's lying." I hesitated, and asked, "Are they still in the same hotel?"

"Nope. Not sure where they are. I'd suggest leaving the investigation to the authorities."

"I'll track them down myself, if you're not going to tell me."

"Unless something comes up during the investigation…"

"I tell you, Wanda Brown has them." I fumed. "Goodbye."

Since it was the start of rush hour and I had to drive through downtown traffic, I slipped in a disc, hoping the easy listening tunes would calm my jagged nerves as I drove home. My life has been upside down since the two-day-old murder.

As I started through downtown, I thought of my girlfriend who owns a small motel right near downtown. It was relatively unknown and someplace that Wanda could hide out in without being hounded by the press. I made a quick turn to circle back to the Twin City Motel. I decided against giving Brenda, my motel owner friend, a call because I hated to have her involved should I decide to enter and search Wanda's room. Brenda left for afternoon classes and returned later. I hoped that I wouldn't have to follow them and stake them out.

The seed of an idea began to germinate as I drove near the hotel. *Hmm…How can I find out which room they were registered in? Did I need a room key? Was there a dining room where I might accidentally brush against her or find the dolls left on her table?* I decided to start at the top of my game plan list and work down until they were back in my possession. Glancing in the rearview mirror, I applied fresh lipstick and captured my wanton set of springy red curls in a headband. I wished I'd worn something classier today, but I held my head high as I stepped out of the car. At the front desk, I set my bag down and smiled sweetly.

"Hello. I'm here to see…" When the desk clerk gazed at me, I began to wonder if this wasn't a stupid idea. *Steady, I told myself. Stay calm.* "I'm here to—."

"Yes, ma'am. How can I help you?" the perky young lady behind the desk finally asked. Her bleached-blonde, spiked hair and nose ring matched, as did the five gold earrings she wore in each ear. She jingled. I thought of the Twelve Days of Christmas.

"Hi! I'm here from Hollywood to take a look at the room where the two leading suspects are staying, Wanda Brown and Stone Rogers. We're thinking about making a movie about her demise, calling it Presidentress Jackie!"

"What on earth are you talking about? A movie?" Her eyes opened wide. "They're here?"

"Look it up."

"They are here." She stared at me.

"Don't you want to be in pictures? Your name will be right on the top."

"I was an actress in high school and always wanted to live in Hollywood."

"Now's your chance," I said. *I struck paydirt with this girl.*

"Really?" Her eyes opened wide.

"Of course. Could you please tell me her room number?" I smiled sweetly and hoped my dimples showed.

"Do you think Brad Pitt would play the bodyguard?"

"He might, but then… let's see—," I said, cocking my head. "You'd fit the part of Jackie. You're tall, aren't you?" The phone rang and the desk clerk answered it, holding up a finger motioning for me to wait. When she hung up, I said, "You'd be perfect with the bodyguard. What a hunk, eh?"

"I can't tell you the room number, but I know for certain that they have nightcaps each afternoon during happy hour—3–5." She nodded toward a distant elevator, and said, "The bar's right down over there. Good luck."

"Thanks. It'll be our secret. I'll be back with Brad tomorrow."

"Okay." Her cheeks were rosy red.

I marched out the front door with my heart pounding. Back in the car, I wondered what to do next. I glanced at the clock. It was almost six, and I needed to beat it home.

No sooner had I walked into the house when Aaron came up beside me and whispered in my ear, "Tonight?"

"There's always hope." I snagged a bottle of wine from the refrigerator while he removed glasses from the cabinet. "Your friends interrogated the three of us today." I marched out of the kitchen and toward the office.

Seated on one chair was Grandpa. Grandma made room on the settee for me as Aaron set the glasses down next to the wine bottle, which I'd placed on the small table. Grandpa made the move to open it. After pouring, he passed around the glasses.

"Here's to Liv." Grandpa raised his glass, and they all followed, "To Liv."

Tears sprang into my eyes while I thought of how much these people loved me.

"Shall we get started?" Aaron took control of the meeting from behind the desk. "Alarm system?"

"The bill is right here. They need a down payment before starting." I removed the paper from my pocket and placed it in Grandpa's opened hand. "I can't afford this. How about if I pay you later?"

"I'll take care of it."

"Cleaners?" Aaron typed on the keyboard before he looked at me.

"Came and gone. Ruth and Suzy. Two older women. Very professional—wonderful job—but they reminded me of Swedish babushka's. The wood floor still needs looking after. The blood soaked into grooves in the wood, and you can still see it in several places. The table that the house was sitting on either needs replacing or painting because the blood soaked into its legs. Actually, it still kind of stinks too, so let's get rid of it." *That was my news flash. Now I hoped that I could think about the hotel and getting back my dolls without being caught. I'll be honest with the credit card company, and remove them from the bill.*

"Okay. Cleaners are checked off the list, but I will add a floor work crew," Aaron said.

"Good grief! It'll take forever to get it all set back to rights," I said.

"It won't be much longer," Grandma said. "Another couple of days."

"There's got to be a reason behind them keeping the dolls. It has to pertain to the 'secret'. I'm positive," I said.

"But, what?" Grandma asked. "What's the secret?"

"I called Detective Erlandsen and he said Wanda claims she doesn't have the dolls. She's lying."

"I wish we knew more." Grandpa drained his glass of wine. "What do the police say?" He looked at Aaron. "What can you tell us?"

"Yes. Please tell, Aaron." Grandma spoke up. "Who are the suspects? What happened to that woman and bodyguard?"

"I'm not part of the investigation, but the two are under suspicion. Let's leave it at that." Aaron looked at me. "Everyone is a suspect."

"Thanks. Now I know why the cops hammered us with questions today. I thought Dorrie was going to quit. They questioned Max too. I don't know what to think, myself." I finished my drink. "But what I don't like is that Jackie took the dolls in such an underhanded way. That's at the core of all of this, I believe. When we figure that out, we might have a motive."

"Let's get back on track." Aaron turned back to the computer. "Last night, we ended our discussion with finding the article about the Montpelier break-in. August, you mentioned that your family came from that area before moving to Minnesota, correct?" He looked back to Grandpa, who nodded. "What does your family tree have to do with the Madisons?"

"The answer is right in here." Grandma reached over to the large Bible sitting on the corner of the desk, and set it between us. "Grandpa's relation was a Putnam."

# Chapter Seven

"Through all of this, you really didn't know that you were a Putnam? The name of the doctor whom Dolley had given the cufflinks, so many years ago? Yikes." I knocked my forehead in jest. "How could you not know that you're related?"

"I don't sit and read the family Bible," Grandpa stated. "As a matter of fact, it's been years since it was dragged out." Grandpa yawned and looked at Grandma. "Bed?"

"Now that you know, we're going to bed."

"What next?" I said, watching them leave the room.

"My sarge needs me to work, honey," Aaron said. "They're short-shifted."

"Shoot!"

"I know. I'll text later to see what you've found out." Aaron kissed me and left.

When he left, I went downstairs to Grandpa's wine cellar to fetch a bottle. I hated going downstairs. I hate basements and the cellar most especially because you have to turn the light on once inside of it. Once I'd picked up a bottle, I went back upstairs.

With a glass of wine in hand, I plugged the Mitch Miller DVD from Mikal into the player. I'd wanted to watch it since he gave it to me—now was my chance. I carried the Bible over to the chair and began leafing through the pages. Mitch's choir sang *You Are My Sunshine*, while the ball bounced on the screen under the song lyrics. As I dove deeper into the pages of Grandpa's Bible, I found his name listed under the names of his parents, along with his siblings, who were deceased. Grandma had entered their birth and the dates of their deaths. Searching further, I found that Grandpa's great-grandpa was a Putnam, with the first name of Elijah. I jotted down the dates and his other information before closing the book. When I glanced up at the TV, I saw that the program was over. I shut it off and went to place the Bible on the cabinet near the First Lady dolls.

Later, I showered, and then stood under the attic trapdoor and peered up at it. It had been ages since I'd been up there to explore. It seemed a lifetime ago since Maggie, a friend from childhood, Dorrie, and I went up there to play. Maggie opened old boxes, filled with letters. We'd heard Grandma holler up at us and tell us not to snoop in the letters, only the trunks. We quickly had closed the box. I barely remembered what was in the trunks. I did recall the large, old Victorian-style women's hats and Victorian dresses, which we played in. An old birdcage stood in the back corner, looking out of place, and I wondered if it was still there? But, why wouldn't it be since no one went up there?

I clicked off the hall light, went into my room, and crawled into bed. My mind was filled with Mitch Miller marching songs with the ball that bounced over the words.

❦

Grandma's singing, *I'm Looking Over a Four Leaf Clover* woke me. Her high-pitched voice was like an alarm clock. In my mind I pictured Mitch Miller's bouncing ball while hoping that it wouldn't stick in my mind.

When dressed, I found my earrings on top of my dresser beside two miniature dollhouses, which I'd considered showcasing in the store. I hadn't found a suitable arrangement for them, and so decided to wait. Aaron buzzed me, and I answered him back. We planned to meet for a bagel at the Loon Cafe nearby before he went to bed, and I to work.

After Grandpa handed me the check for the security team, I gave him a smooch, and headed out the door.

Aaron was already parked in the Loon's lot when I parked beside it. He saw me pull up and gave me a kiss as we entered the café.

I sat at a cozy booth while he picked up our orders. As he slid in beside me, we kissed again.

"When do you get a night off?" I leaned into him and drew in a deep breath. I wanted all of him. "I'm lonesome." I spread strawberry jam on my bagel and took a bite.

"I know, baby. Next week we rotate shifts." He reached for his bagel and spread cream cheese on it. "I have something to tell you, but you have to stay calm." He drank his orange juice.

"Now what?" This didn't sound good. "Give it to me straight."

"Wanda Brown flat out denies having the dolls and claims that Jackie never took them. There's no cause for a search warrant because there's no evidence working against her."

"She is lying because I have the credit card receipt. I don't stand a chance in getting them back, do I?"

"Sorry about that, I wish there was something I could do to help you out, but there isn't." Aaron placed his arm over my shoulder and pulled me close.

"I know she took those two dolls—I saw it. Why would Wanda lie about this? Do you think she had something to do with Jackie's death?" I glanced up at the clock. "I'd better get to work. The remaining houses need to be moved out before the floor people begin working. Grandma is arranging the work crew." I thought of drinking down the remainder of the juice, but decided against it. "By the way, I found Grandpa's name and Elijah Putnam's in the family Bible."

"Talk about coincidences." Aaron cocked his head and looked at me.

"I don't believe in coincidences."

"Have you had time to dig out the cufflinks?"

"No," I said, shaking my head. "Not since Grandma and Grandpa's anniversary. There are a couple of pictures that I could take a closer look at." I frowned. "How does this fit into the investigation? The cufflinks. Dorrie might be right. The sampler is a little odd. It might have clues, too." I sighed. "All known facts are disjointed."

"How true, but it has to lead to the motive, then all questions will be answered." Aaron yawned, then kissed my forehead. "I'm going to bed. The graveyard shift is enough to do anyone in."

We went our separate ways. I wondered if it helped or hindered my case to have a fiancé on the police force, because I felt more out of sorts. It didn't take long before I parked and entered the back door, flipping on the lights. Dorrie was right—the scent of blood was faintly evident.

"Morning, girls! I'll be out there in a minute-and-a-half," I called to the dolls.

I definitely was not ready for new customers. I plunked in a CD of Christmas music even though it was still a few weeks away. The first song was *White Christmas* sung by Bing Crosby. I began humming along as he crooned, "I'm dreaming of a…", while entering the showroom.

"Look at you, Mrs. Hoover, all dressed up for the inauguration. I bet you're more comfortable in your outdoor get-up, aren't you?" I smiled at her then moved on to Mrs. Carter. "You're lookin' good, so's Mr. Carter. Rosalynn and Jimmy, sitting on a tree, k-i-s-s-i-n-g!"

I headed to the computer. While the computer hummed through its login script, I sang *White Christmas*. I had forgotten some of the words. *Wish I could see that bouncing ball like on the Mitch Miller program.* Finally, the desktop appeared on the monitor, and I clicked on the Internet browser's icon. *Back to digging into Jackie Newell's personal life.* I googled Jackie and several sites appeared. Perusing the links, eventually I learned that she was a highly requested speaker, mostly on savvy, popular trends and the buying public. At last I found a listing of her speaking engagements over the previous six months. My heart pounded as I stared at the screen. She'd spoken at a convention near the Montpelier Estate the day before the heist.

*Why did Jackie Newell steal Dolley's jewelry?*

Next, I searched the web for Elijah Putnam and learned that at one time he'd been a medical doctor and lived near the Madisons. He was younger than Madison, making it highly possible that Putnam had been his doctor. Since money was a grave issue for Dolley, she certainly could have bequeathed the cufflinks to Mr. Putnam upon Mr. Madison's death as a payment for services rendered.

*I was starting to see a beginning, but the trail was mystifying.*

As I clicked out of the site, voices from the back of the shop caught my attention.

"Right over here." Max clopped into the showroom with the security team close behind. "The lady has the check, right?"

"You bet. My bag's in the back. Hold on a sec." I jumped up and skirted past the men. I removed the check from my bag and handed it to the man with the outstretched hand. I'd forgotten their names. "Give me the final bill when you're finished." They set to work.

Max hadn't moved. "Well? When's August coming over to help?"

"Grandpa? Anytime. He was reading the paper and eating when I left home."

"Ahh—retirement." He started walking away, then stopped. "I'll start carrying the houses into the back room, and with any luck we won't have to carry them all up to the apartment. We'll see."

"You're a treasure, Max. Thanks." I no sooner responded to another customer requesting a set of Madison dolls, when three people entered the store. I walked over toward them.

"We're kind of a mess right now to be open for business," I said. "I do have catalogues if you don't see what you'd like."

"I want a Dolley Madison house."

"I don't have one on display to show you," I said. "You'd have to look in the—"

"Right here," a woman dashed to the vacant area. "Look!" She glanced downward.

The other two women followed right behind.

"Is this where it was?" a woman asked, looking down at the spot.

"How may I help you?" I asked, slightly annoyed.

"I still want a house," the first woman said.

"Right over here, and I'll make the sale. Follow me to the counter, please." I texted Max. "Cash or credit card?" The two women stayed back. "Right over here, please."

"This is right where she landed. See that? Blood splattered on the table legs." Two of the three women walked over to the counter, finally.

"How will you pay? Cash or credit?"

My head was spinning as more people entered through the front door. I heard footsteps from the backroom, and was relieved to see Max enter.

Max quickly ushered the spectators out of the store, and turned to the women before me. "You want a Madison house?"

"Yes. I'm paying for one," the woman pushed her glasses further on her nose.

"Where are you parked?"

"Right out the door."

"I'll carry the boxes out."

After taking care of the sale and Max finished, I glanced at my inbox once again, and there were already five more orders for a Madison house. People also wanted to know if Jackie's brain gushed out all over. I deleted the gruesome messages.

I presumed Max planned to make room across the workbench and countertops for the houses, but didn't think they'd all fit. The houses were large. In its early years, the White House was smaller simply because the additions hadn't happened. In the newer dollhouse styles, features were added such as the Rose Garden, which is always a beautiful attraction and selling point.

Supervising the shifting of the dollhouses shot my sorting project for the day, but I was close to being done, and my assigned investigation was completed. Grandma's job was to locate the floor crew. I heard Grandpa's voice in the back of the shop, so I went to meet them.

"You came, too?" I asked. Grandma stood to the right of Grandpa. "Great."

"Just wanted to check things out and make sure that my grand-daughter doesn't need any help." She glanced at the shelves and noticed that the boxes were stacked, labeled neatly, and trimmed. "You're all caught up."

"Pretty much. I haven't sewn the Dolley dresses, though. I thought since you were coming, that I'd leave you to mind the store while I go to a fabric store to purchase what I needed to sew the dresses. Sometimes I'm lucky and find the buff colored material in town, otherwise I have to order it. I have several orders waiting to fill at the moment. Do you mind?"

"No. I'll stay for the rest of the day. Go ahead."

"Thanks. Have you contacted the floor crew?"

"Yes, dear." Grandma eyes blinked, I knew she had something up her sleeve. "One of the book club ladies knows someone who refinishes floors. All of my lady friends from the book club are trustworthy, so I'm sure the two men she referred me to will be perfect."

Grandma's explanation left me a little edgy. "What's the name?"

"Name of what?" Grandma giggled.

My gut flip-flopped. "The work crew."

She inhaled deeply. "The Two Jims."

"Two Jims?" There's nothing wrong with two men named Jim, I told myself. "Why are you giggling?"

"They'll be fine. Remember now, they were recommended by the book clubbers."

"Oh my stars. What are their last names?" Max asked.

"One Jim is a Tew." Grandma looked me straight in the eye. "The other is Flowers."

"This is beginning to sound like that Abbott and Costello skit, 'Who's on first?'" Max winked at me and nodded to Grandpa. "Well, ladies, August and I have plenty to do if you want to get the tables and houses out of the showroom before they arrive."

"See you back home." I grabbed my coat and bag. While climbing into my car, my thoughts went to the hotel. It was now or never to get the dolls. I needed a disguise.

Perfect timing. The store isn't open for business and I'm unneeded. I reflected as I crossed the bridge over the Mississippi and drove into the downtown shopping district. Before long I was turning into a small parking lot.

I raced across the street to the five-and-dime store and found a brown, long straight-haired wig. I thought it best to look for a different top. I chose a frilly one that sparkled with sequins, making me feel like a dancer. The bright red color went with my white jeans. Now all I was needed were some dangly earrings, which I purchased with the other items.

Now I had my happy hour costume.

I found the bathroom at the five and dime, and slipped into my new outfit.

Back in the car, I used a marker to draw a tiny heart on my ankle to finish the costume, then I shut off my phone before climbing out of the car. *A noisy phone while stealing back my dolls from a killer would not be smart.*

Out on the street, I decided to stand to the side and watch and wait, and hope that a cleaning lady or two dressed in uniform would walk past so that I could follow them inside. I glanced at my watch. Another five minutes went by, and I watched two women wearing Twin City Motel uniforms stomp out their cigarettes.

"Hey there! When's happy hour?" I rushed up and started talking. I hadn't wanted to enter alone. "Heard that Brad Pitt's here."

"Really?" The gal wearing tattoos for sleeves looked at me. "I ain't seen him." They went into the elevator and I kept going toward the bar.

The clinking of glass plus murmuring voices propelled me further until at last coming to the dark room. Several individuals lined the bar while couples sat side by side around tables. On top of tables were candles, some lit. I looked around the room, but didn't see the two I searched for. I decided to order from the bartender and sit in a far off corner to wait and see if they'd arrive or not.

As I sipped my drink, I wish I knew if Wanda Brown and the bodyguard, Stone Rogers, were still in their rooms, and if they were together. The wig made me warm, and sweat beads dotted my forehead and brow. *Where were they?* My heart skipped a beat as I watched the couple enter and stop near the bar. There they were.

Keeping my eye on them, I moved slightly closer without them noticing. Eventually, they moved to a table nearby, their voices rising. The way she clutched the purse so close to her chest, led me to believe that the dolls were locked inside of it.

"I tell you, we have to leave this town. The police are getting closer," Stone said.

"Those dolls. They keep asking about them. I can't afford to leave them in the hotel room anymore. What if they get a search warrant," Wanda said.

"That damn shopkeeper, Liv. Whatever her name is. Where are they now?" Stone asked.

"Right in my purse. Then I'll always know where they are," Wanda said.

"Let me look at them again. Maybe there's something we're missing," he said.

"You never know," she said, taking them out. "Here." She grabbed her purse, and said, "I'll be right back."

*Yes! They are in her purse.*

It was my cue. I waited a moment, knowing full well that she'd go to the bathroom. It didn't take long before I was right beside Stone. As I tried to figure out how to get my hands on the dolls, an opportunity arose. The waitress carried a tray with two drinks on top started in our direction. When she was close by, I slid my chair out as she reached over to set the drinks down. Instantly, the drink tipped over and Stone was covered with the beverage.

"Stupid woman," he said, standing up.

"Sorry," she replied.

"Here's my napkin," I said, handing it over. In the confusion I hid the two dolls within my palm and hurried out the room.

As I walked, the voices behind me rose. In the hallway, Wanda approached, causing me to avert my eyes.

As soon as she turned into the room, I stuffed the dolls into my bag. I took the back way, exiting out the side door and racing to my car.

Once inside the car, I hadn't realized that my heart was racing and my fingers shaking as I stuck the key into the ignition. I opened the bag and peered at the dolls. Mr. and Mrs. Madison looked brand new. I stuck the key in the engine and began my drive home.

# Chapter Eight

The house was empty. As I leaned against the closed kitchen door, my heart was still beating like a drum. I shut my eyes as my mind replayed the last hour. When I'd come to grips with the situation, I went straight to the office and turned on the light over Grandpa's desk, before plunking down on the chair. I pulled the dolls out of my bag, setting them carefully on the desk.

"Well, little Dolley and James, I aim to get to the bottom of this little escapade of yours, even if it's the last thing that I do!" I removed the magnifying glass from the desk drawer and picked up the James doll. A framed picture of my grandparents on their anniversary was on the desk. I zeroed in on Grandpa's cufflinks. I picked up the doll and inspected it with the magnifying glass before setting it down.

I was positive they were a match.

A gold gadroon encircled all three, the two cufflinks and Dolley's brooch. The cufflinks set had sapphires, diamonds, and rubies, set to look like a waving flag exactly like the pictured brooch. Unfortunately, the gadroon imprint was too tiny to read.

Leaning back in the chair, the word "coincidence" went through my mind. Another one. There were so many. I slid the picture back inside the frame and put the magnifier back in the drawer. The dolls needed to be hidden, but where? And the next question begged for asking. *Are the cufflinks still in the little pocket like Grandpa said?*

For the time being, I wrapped the dolls in tissue, and shoved aside the cigar box, which covered the carved rose wood block on the desktop. I pressed into it and waited for the latch to pop before lifting the rose plate out. I peered inside. A small jewelry box lay at the bottom of the compartment and I pulled it out. Upon opening it, I gasped and dropped into the chair. The cufflinks had been secreted away all these years right under my nose, and never knew it until a few days ago.

*Is my life in danger because of the cufflinks?*

The barely readable gadroon read: *Polly.* For the life of me, I couldn't make sense of it. *Who was Polly?*

After quite awhile of trying to make sense out of the find, I set the dolls plus the cufflinks back down into the hidden pocket, closing it up.

I went to the refrigerator, took out two small sodas, then headed out the door. I crossed over the snow-dusted yard, climbed Aaron's back steps, and knocked on his back door. When he didn't answer, I yanked out my keys and unlocked it.

"Honey?" I called while entering. I hated waking him, but we needed to discuss the cufflinks. I found him sleeping and whispered in his ear. I glanced at the clock. Since it was mid-afternoon, I knew that he'd soon awaken without my help. I kissed his cheek and tickled his ear causing him to open an eye.

"Hmm." He grabbed me.

"I, ahh, have some exciting news to tell you." He began kissing me all over, and we spent time reacquainting ourselves.

A while later, we were out in the kitchen where I had left the sodas. Aaron popped open the cans, handing mine over. "Well, so what news do you have to tell me?"

"It's like this… There's another huge coincidence," I said, looking closely at him.

"Tell me. Speak up." He took a gulp from his can. "I know. You saw the two somewhere, dressed like bums. They spotted you and chased you down the street—and you barely got away."

"Hush now!" Aaron always made me giggle. "Almost. I put on a wig, changing my looks." I cleared my throat, "I went to the bar lounge in the hotel to wait for Stone and Wanda. Would you believe they entered? The waitress spilled drinks on Stone who had been holding the dolls. You won't believe this, but—."

"You took them? I never believed that you'd do that. We have to call the detectives right now." He gave me a concerned look.

"You're right. I will." I sipped my soda and took a moment to piece my thoughts together. I left a message on Erlandsen's phone, relaying to him about the dolls. Afterwards, I told Aaron about the remarkable resemblance between Grandpa's cufflinks and the painted ones on the doll. "They were right where he said they'd be. In the desk pocket."

"I know they want me to wear them for our wedding too."

"It seems likely." I thought for a moment. "Also, there's the gadroon that says 'Polly', which we need to find out about. I found out that Grandpa's great-grandpa was named Elijah Putnam. More coincidences that circle the Madisons." I shook my head. "It's mind boggling."

"Who are we going to share this information with—or will we keep it between us?" Aaron said. "It's soon time for our afternoon meeting, hon."

"Let's keep it between us." I stood, picked up the empty cans, and threw them in Aaron's recycling bin. "I'm not sure if we should let anyone in on the dolls' matching cufflinks. What's there to tell, anyway? We don't have any clues or facts that lead to Wanda or the bodyguard."

"Which leads us nowhere." Aaron reached for his keys. "Let's get over there. August and Marie are waiting."

"You're right. Grandpa and Grandma are holding their breath waiting for us." I ran down Aaron's back steps before zipping back across the yards. When I entered the house, I immediately went downstairs to bring up laundry, walking right beside the wine cellar, which gave me the creeps.

The meeting lasted only a few minutes between us since Grandma and Grandpa had plans for the evening. Aaron had a late shift, so I stayed in my own bed. I was ready to face the day when morning came, and hurried to work.

One of my tasks for the day was to supervise the Two Jims. I'd picked up the downtown newspaper when I stopped for coffee and a roll.

"It's so empty in the showroom." I thought of my mother. She'd always told me to keep my chin up and all would be well with the world. I missed her something fierce. I pasted on a smile.

Sitting by the computer counter, I spread the newspaper out, and then glanced at the photo on the front page. I sipped my steaming coffee and leaned in closer for a better view of the lead article, the one with a headline reading, *The murderer is yet to be found.*

My mouth dropped open. Right below the headline was a picture of the two thieves. I plunked the coffee down on the counter. My mind spun as I gave the photos a closer look. "Pshaw! The police are onto them, but are they the killers? Anyway, they'll be jailed soon." When I finished the article, I found that Ronnie was the reporter.

As I swallowed the last bite of my roll, the Jims entered. Both wore striped shirts under hooded sweatshirts, khaki pants and leather boots. I shook hands with the tallest Jim first. "I'm Liv." I said, and he pumped my arm so hard that I wondered if it would fall off.

"Just call me Slim." His smile revealed a missing front tooth, and his huge, puppy dog eyes reminded me of a pet cocker spaniel that we used to have.

"Call me Jim." The second Jim smiled, his eyes twinkling. He was about my height. With his cap removed, his pointed bald head stuck up like a sharp point. I sucked the inside of my cheek to stifle a laugh.

"Let me show you around." I nodded toward the bathroom and touched the storage room door. "This room is off limits."

At the previous evening's meeting, Max told me that the tables were folded and stacked against the side wall. He'd also covered the sewing table, the counters, and the workbench. All of the dollhouses were upstairs in his apartment.

"Follow me." I waved my hand and headed into the showroom. "This floor needs the stripping."

"Sounds good," Jim said.

"We'll get the sanders," Slim said.

They turned and began marching out. Slim suddenly stopped and Jim plowed into him. "What have I always told you?" Slim said over his shoulder.

"Yah, well, don't stop so sudden like." Jim flipped off his cap, then sat it back down.

I shook my head and looked away. This day was going to prove itself to be entertaining, I reckoned, as I went back to the computer and covered it in plastic.

The whir of two sanding machines, plus all the dust, forced me into the workroom. I was eager to research Dolley Madison and Polly. I gave Aaron a call.

"You sleeping?" *Poor guy—he'll be a zombie because of the hours he has to work.* I disconnected when he said that he'd bring his laptop down for me to use. I tucked away my phone, and got up to check on the two Jims. The sander noise had stopped, and I heard the door close.

Stepping into the room, I found it empty.

"Oh my goodness. Now where are they?" I walked to the front door and looked out the window, but didn't see them. They'd vanished. I went to open the backdoor and saw them sitting in a van with two women. "What the heck?" I opened the door and was just ready to call out when they turned in my direction. Instantly, they shot across the street and started their explanations.

"Our wives. They brought us an early lunch."

"Get to work, boys." I blew the hair from my face as I went back to the workroom once I felt secure that they'd get back to work.

I sat down before pulling the *Historical Homes* magazine out of my bag. It wasn't easy to concentrate with all the noise and annoyances. It was only half past ten, and I already felt as if I'd put in a full day's work. I locked the door.

The back door opened a few minutes later.

"I'm in here," I said to Max.

"Noisy. Yikes." He stood by the doorway and stared inward.

"I'll say. That's why I'm in here." I frowned, wishing the day was over.

"Did you lock the door?"

"No, I suppose that I should've," Max stated. "Just a sec."

"I'm getting a headache from all of this." I knew he'd be securing the door.

"I can see why." He cocked his head. "I saw someone last night hovering near the entrance, and the sensor lights went on and off." Max looked at me squarely. "I think they're getting serious."

"You're saying that someone tried to break in again? The police need to know about this. What about the new alarm system?" I stared at him. "There's nothing here. What could they be after?"

"These people mean business." Max dropped into the nearest chair. "You must have something that they want, even if you don't know what it is. Jackie was after the dolls and got them. Did you ever get them back?"

"Yes, but don't tell anyone. Not even Dorrie. I'm calling the police." I called it in and told the desk sergeant about the possible break-in from last night. "The detectives will be told. Any further questioning needed they'll contact us."

"Hey! Just checking in," Aaron called as he entered. "What's up?"

"A possible break-in last night."

Max looked seriously at me. "I've got things to do. I plan to catch up on the doll head carvings. I'm behind with Eleanor Roosevelt."

"I'll call the desk sergeant, and he'll pass on the message."

"Wait a minute." Aaron gave me a puzzled look. "Didn't anyone get a call from security?'

"Nothing happened. I saw two figures outside, but then they left. I never got a chance to call because they left right away. I've got to get busy. You two figure it out." Max stood with his hand on the doorknob.

"Interesting." Aaron shook his head. "The police are still interviewing today."

"Oh yeah?" I perked up. "Who?"

"Don't know for sure what's happening. I'm not in the loop. It'll be over soon. Just be patient."

"Patient, you say? What's that?" I was about ready to reach into Dolley's grave and yank her out by her feathered turban.

# Chapter Nine

Loud voices boomed from behind the closed workroom door.

"Yes?" Aaron got up, and opened it.

"Liv?" Slim lowered his eyes. "The floor... well...." He cleared his throat.

"What he's trying to say is that it's done." Jim stood straight. "We've put a layer of polyurethane on it, so don't walk on it."

I got up and walked over to Aaron, who placed his arm around my waist and pulled me close.

"Take a look." Slim stepped aside.

We followed them to the showroom, and stopped. The floor glistened, and looked brand new. "It's beautiful. Absolutely gorgeous."

"We'll be back in the morn to add another coat."

"How many coats are you doing?" Aaron asked, just as his phone rang, which he answered. I watched him frown, and slip it into his pocket.

"Once more should do it. It'll shine like a newborn baby's—"

"Hush, now!"

I giggled. I couldn't help it. "Okay. See you about ten. Right?"

"Yes, ma'am."

I watched them leave and locked the back door. The smell of the polyurethane started to give me a headache. I gave Max a call and told him that they were finished for the day, and warned him that it would be like this for another day.

"Hon?" I stood with my bag in hand, eyes on Aaron.

"I have an appointment. I'll call you when I can."

"I'll be fine." I went out to fetch the mail after he'd left. I zipped through the few pieces and shoved them into my bag. I thought of those cufflinks and knew they'd better be put in a safer place. I walked out to my car and climbed in. My thoughts went to the gadroon and the word, Polly.

*And what was the secret that Jackie had referred to? I knew that I'd soon have to go to the University library and spend time researching through old history books. There had to be something that I'd missed when working on my doctoral.*

Puzzled, I drove home.

As I walked up to the house, my mind went over the research I'd done about Dolley Madison. Once inside, I quickly locked the door. A note on the table read:

> *A) Hairdresser:*
> *B) Grocery shopping:*
> *C) Home.*

I glanced at the calendar where Grandma usually made notes ,and found the answer was *A*—one o'clock hairdresser appointment, *B* and *C* followed right after.

It was now after two. I had little time alone and planned to make the most of it. I took the envelope from my bag and headed into the den.

I fetched the dolls and cufflinks from the hidden rose pocket because they needed a better hiding place. Since I didn't have a personal safe box I couldn't bring them to the bank. I brought the stool from my room closet over to the attic opening, and set it down. The opening roughly measured two feet by three. I stepped on the stool and pulled the cord to drop the attic stairs. I wasn't sure what I'd find up there, and hoped the light bulb hadn't burned out.

I pulled the string and dim light illuminated the small room. Two small trunks sat off to one side. Large hatboxes were stacked on the other side, with smaller boxes in front of them. Plenty of cobwebs as well as dust, covered everything. I sneezed. My old rocking horse and a large box full of old dolls sat in the forefront. In a far corner sat an old, rickety birdcage surrounded by Victorian-style women's shoes. I made my way over to the birdcage for a closer inspection. The bottom was covered with old newspaper, but the birdseed and water holders were relatively clean. For the life of me, I couldn't imagine where this cage had come from. Underneath it was a small drawer, so I slid it open.

"Perfect." I set the dolls and cufflinks in the bottom of the drawer and closed it. I placed the birdcage back in the corner and carefully replaced the shoes, setting them exactly as before. If someone snooped, the displacement of dust wouldn't be evident.

After shutting off the light, I started back down the attic stairs and closed up the hatch door. I checked to be sure it was closed tight and the latches were in their worn grooves. I set the stool back in the closet and stacked a pile of dirty laundry over it.

I heard Grandma and Grandpa entering the back door. I took a minute, just to let my mind rest, and then walked down the stairs to find them unloading the groceries.

"Aaron called. Your phone must be turned off." Grandma smiled at me. "He said for me to tell you to get dressed up. He's taking you out to dinner."

"Oh. He didn't say anything about that earlier." I opened a can of soda and watched them sort through the grocery bags. I knew I should've helped, but they had some kind of system between them, whereas I always seemed to get in their way. Experience took over, I realized sitting down. "What time?"

"Five. He was on his way to gas up, but he's probably home by now," Grandpa said.

"Thanks." I took a swallow. I was excited to be alone with Aaron.

"You look nervous." Grandma gave me a quick study. "A little peaked."

"Headache from all the noise and dust." I took a deep breath. "I have the dolls. The cufflinks match your set from in the hidden desk pocket, which are now upstairs in the attic."

"They were fine right where they were," Grandpa said.

"No, they weren't. They need to be in a bank deposit box. There are too many unanswerable questions and coincidences happening recently pertaining to the Madisons. If there's anything else that you haven't told me about the Putnams, now is the time."

"The cufflinks have never been a secret with us nor the Putnams," Grandma said, with tear filled eyes. "My cousin, the one we spoke of the other day? She passed away, and the attorney has a box of letters waiting for me to pick up. We're going to St. Paul tomorrow to get them."

"Another coincidence. What's her name?"

"Nellie. She's from my mother's side, which means that she's also a Dolley relative," Grandma said.

"I wonder what's in the letters? They might be interesting. I wonder what they'll say? Now, I'm going to shower and get myself spiffed up." I walked away.

Up in my room, I texted Aaron to find out what I should wear

He wanted me in that '*sx blk drs*'—which meant that he wanted me in that sexy black dress.

I giggled as I fetched it from the closet and laid it out on the bed before jumping into the shower. We'd been a couple for so long, that he'd asked me to marry him in high school. After applying makeup and nail polish, I did my best with my unruly, curly-cue red hair, pulling it back with ringlets accentuating my face. I slipped into the dress and matching black dress shoes, and pulled my sequined black purse from a drawer.

When I descended the stairs, I was met by the threesome.

Aaron smiled and kissed me, and his eyes lit up like the national Christmas tree in front of the White House. He kissed Grandma, too.

Hand in hand, we walked across the shoveled path to his car. When inside, we kissed each other deeply. "Where to?"

"One of those fancy places on 494, or would you rather go to a neighborhood restaurant?" He kissed me again, then started the engine.

"Neighborhood, and Italian."

"Bella's, here we come!" His eyes sparkled, and his breathing seemed slightly faster than normal when my hand fell onto his leg. Within a few minutes, we were parking and he was opening my car door.

My mind seemed to spin out of control all night. The candles and champagne bubbles glimmered like diamonds in the dimly lit room. I had trouble following Aaron's words as he placed the engagement ring on my finger.

"Right before Christmas. What do ya say?"

"Perfect," I softly breathed.

A piano man played romantic songs all night as we stared into each other's eyes. Glancing around the room, I was very proud of my man as I saw lovers doing the same. Tears of joy spilled down my blushing cheeks. As the restaurant's decorative lights dimmed and candles on the tables snuffed, we strolled to the car, arm in arm.

Aaron kept me warm all night.

I woke beside him, smiling. I headed home to shower and get ready for work. Since I had to be at work before ten to let in the Two Jims, there wasn't time to spare. I also wanted to get some time in before the dust and smell gave me a headache. While driving, my thoughts went to Polly. *Who is Polly?* I parked in my usual spot, but felt creepy, and my skin tingled.

For some reason, I had the feeling that I was being spied upon so I locked the store door behind me. As a start, I'd find a place to hide my bag. All the shelves were too visible in the backroom. Under the counter would be too apparent. I settled on the bathroom cabinet, and stuffed my bag behind the toilet paper, hand towels, and tissue boxes. As soon as I shut the door there was rapping. I let the Jims enter.

"We're here," Slim stated.

"Mornin'." Jim went into the workroom to carry out the polyurethane plus the needed application equipment. "Let's get started, Slim."

"You betcha!" Slim headed toward the showroom. The three of us stopped just short of entering to admire the shine.

"Sure is shiny," I softly said.

"Uff da! Let's get to work now, Slim."

"You betcha!"

I waited a few minutes and then went next door to visit Mikal. I was eager to show him my engagement ring.

Mikal was just stepping inside his small office, and I followed him. "We figured out a date."

"Good. About time." He smiled. "Finally. When is the big day? I want an invitation, if I may?"

"Of course. We're inviting only a few people. Grandma and I have to go shopping for flowers. Grandpa already has a tux. It's just Aaron who needs one."

"You still didn't say when, my dear." He grinned, holding onto the back of his chair. "I need to write it into my calendar."

"Oh. Right. Week before Christmas. Three weeks away."

"You can get a minister that soon, plus make all of the other wedding arrangements?" Mikal's eyes were opened wide as he chuckled. "Do you already have your dress?" He narrowed his eyes and stared at me. "Bet you do?"

"Of course. Grandma has her dress too. I'm wearing my mother's dress, in her honor." Tears sprang into my eyes. "I only need a bouquet. I haven't told my best friend, Maggie, yet. She probably won't be surprised though, since Aaron and I have dated for years."

"I'm honored to be the first one you've told." He gave me a big hug before I left.

"Toodles," I called over my shoulder and went out the door.

A now familiar and strong odor greeted me as I stepped back into my shop. I peeked into the showroom and found the Two Jims working hard. Dust filtered through the air, and I went back to the workroom. *Now I really had a lot to do!* First, I called the minister,

Pastor Dahl, and set up a meeting for later in the afternoon. He wrote the wedding date on the church calendar—December 19. I gave Maggie a call, and we arranged to meet Saturday to look at bridesmaid dresses. With Grandma, I discussed the guest list—we decided on twenty people.

I perused the Internet on my iPad for the next few hours in search of wedding invitation styles. I also paged through a bridal magazine I had purchased, gathering catering and decorating ideas. When I heard voices approaching, I clicked out of the iPad and met the Two Jims near the door.

"We're finished, if you want to take a look?"

"Will do!" Together we walked to the entrance and my mouth dropped open. "It's beautiful. I can't thank you enough."

"Just what we wanted to hear," Jim said. "We'll carry out the rest of our equipment, then be gone."

"Should we send the bill or will you pay now?"

"A bill's better with an itemized statement for the insurance company," I said.

"Okay."

"Thanks, guys." I watched them walk out the door with the last of their equipment. I went to look again at the floor, which still amazed me at how smooth and glossy it looked.

I was about to get my bag and leave to fetch myself lunch, when Aaron walked inside, wearing his uniform.

"Hey, love, brought us some wraps loaded with fresh veggies and cheese for lunch, plus bottles of water." He held the bag. "Wonderful."

"It's gorgeous." I knew he meant the ring. Glancing around, I had that feeling again of being watched. I frowned. "I feel like I'm being watched."

"Nothing to worry about. They're being questioned again, Wanda and Stone." Aaron glanced at his watch. "I have ten minutes left." He gave me a quick kiss.

"Really? Maybe something will happen now?"

Aaron nodded at me.

"Find a motive yet?"

"They may let them go. Their attorney is with them and whipping up a storm, so it won't be long and they'll be free to leave."

"Ahh jeez, then it'll be back to square one."

"Everyone is suspect. Everyone will be interrogated again. Remember that." Aaron finished his wrap, and so did I.

"Find out about Polly yet?"

"Not yet, but plan on it. I just forgot because of the Two Jims." I finished my sandwich. "Will you be over tonight?" I asked after we'd picked up the wrappers and bottles, which I threw away.

"Yes. Of course." He kissed me. "Say, have you had time to look through that magazine of historical houses? There's a picture you might find interesting." We stopped near the squad car. "Call me after you've found it."

"Won't you tell me which one?"

"Nope. It must jump out at you, or it won't count." He eyed me closely. "Seriously."

"Really?" I waited until he'd driven away before hustling back inside. "And, they say women are mysterious." I sighed, sitting down. I found Aaron's magazine and opened it up.

Since I wasn't sure what to look for, I skimmed the pages. Nothing caught my eye, so I went back to page one to look closer. Presidential homes were featured in the beginning, starting with Mount Vernon, George Washington's home. I marveled at how well-preserved the house was, which propelled me to keep looking. The homes were featured in order of the presidency, so John Adams' farm in Braintree, Massachusetts was next, Jefferson's Monticello, with many more including Franklin Roosevelt's in Hyde Park and Theodore Roosevelt's in Oyster Bay. I loved looking at all the pictures and it helped pass the time, since I couldn't do anything in the store. Curious, I kept looking.

I wanted to leave so bad, but the doors would be locked and the mailman may not leave the mail. I might miss the wonderful mail order sale. I went back to looking at the magazine photos. For the life of me, I searched for something spectacular, but nothing jumped out at me. I set the magazine aside while glancing into the hallway at all the dust hanging in the air.

Groaning, I reopened the magazine once again. The next section featured homes from *Our Founding Fathers*—those who hadn't already been featured in the presidents' pages.

The first page of this section featured a large photo of Alexander Hamilton's home, the Grange. I learned that it's still located on the original plot of land that once belonged to the family in New York City. The room images were crystal clear, so I peered closer. A parlor wall hanging caught my attention. I wasn't quite certain of the dates on the embroidery. The sampler corners, however, were what captured my attention.

The upper-right had a marigold. The upper left had a rose. The lower left and right each had a marigold. The similarity to Grandma's sampler was unnerving. Shivering, I realized that the hair on my neck tingled. *That Aaron, he knew it matched.*

# Chapter Ten

Just as I was ready to press the button to speed dial Aaron, Max entered. I dropped the phone back into my pocket and shoved the magazine aside. "You surprised me."

"What's that you got there?" Max looked down at the magazine, then back up at me. "Pictures, eh? Thinking about expanding from White Houses to other mansions?" He turned the magazine around for easy viewing.

"What's up?" I wanted to change the subject. "The guys are finished with the floor. Have you seen it yet? It's really nice. It shines like satin sheets." I sucked in my breath, and the lingering smell plus the dust made me cough.

"Not yet, only from a distance." Max studied me with arms crossed, which forced me to paste an innocent look on my face. "You've got something up your sleeve. Fess up."

"I'd like to know how you can always read my mind? I'm just thinking about these pictures, and wishing I could see these homes. The dollhouses need a few more years to get off the ground before I expand. We're a new company."

"Ahh, yes, a new company." Max cleared his throat and jutted out his chin. "At least let me hire the next head carver."

"We would both want to see how fine they cut and how intricate they are with facial lines. It takes a steady hand. Wouldn't want it any other way." Thankfully, at that moment, my cell phone rang. It was Grandma. "Hi Grandma. The floor looks wonderful." I listened as she talked about a schedule change with Pastor Dahl. "Okay, I'll call you right back Grandma." I disconnected. "Let's go look."

"Glad this is done." I started for the showroom with Max following. I didn't want to show him the pictured wall hanging because it's so incredible—another coincidence. "The smell is going to make me sick, if we don't get some ventilation in here."

"It'll clear out soon enough. We can prop open the doors for a few minutes in the morning, but it should dry solid tonight." Max stood for a minute. "Guess you want to leave?"

"I've got things to do, like wedding plans."

"Hmm. Guess that's why you're looking through mansion magazines instead of brides'?"

"Aaron wanted me to look at something." I swept around him and scooped the magazine from the counter. "Gotta run. I'll lock on the way out." I stood by the bathroom door.

"Good."

I grabbed my coat and bag before heading outside without looking back. Once in the car, I speed-dialed Aaron, but got stuck with voice mail and left the message, "A rose? On the wallhanging? It means something, but what?" Next, I called Grandma and found that I was supposed to meet her at the florist in fifteen minutes. The appointment with Pastor Dahl was changed because of a parishioner's death. Grandpa was dropping her off at the florist, and I was supposed to drive her home when it was finished. I headed the car toward south Minneapolis.

Zipping through downtown was only possible in the middle of the night. At this time of day, bumper-to-bumper traffic backed up the roads. It seemed to take forever for the stoplights to turn green. Eventually, I turned onto Cedar where it angled toward Minnehaha Avenue. The florist shop came into view. I turned the corner and parked in the rear.

I hurried inside and found Grandma sitting and paging through a floral album. Approaching, I said, "I want plenty of roses in my bouquet, orchids for the men. Maggie's bouquet must match mine. That's all I care about." I continued, "Can we get married at home? Over Christmas? The house is already so perfectly decorated. It'd be spectacular."

"Now, you bring it up? We have to talk with Grandpa. What about Aaron?" Grandma looked at the florist and said, "I think we'll have to get back to you."

"I just thought of that now. The banister would be lovely clothed in green, lit with tiny lights. Oh, Grandma, it'd be so lovely!"

"We'll call you once the wedding location is settled, but for sure she'll want the bridal party flowers and her bouquet," Grandma said to the florist. Looking at me, she said, "Let's go home where we can discuss this more clearly."

"All right." During the walk to the car, I asked, "What's on your mind?"

"I just ordered sprays for the tables." Grandma's eyes glimmered with tears. "Your mother would insist on having one, and also a pianist for the ceremony."

It was pretty quiet in the car on the way home. Grandma didn't say much of anything, except how pretty it looked outside, and that it was beginning to cloud up, as if a snowstorm was brewing.

I drove into the driveway and shut the engine off.

"You'll make a lovely bride. Your mother would be so proud," Grandma said, bursting into tears. "It'll be fine, dear. I have to speak to Grandpa about something first, but you go ahead and see what Aaron has to say. He may want a church wedding." She climbed from the car and we hurried inside.

"Pastor Dahl won't mind, will he?"

"No. I suspect that he'd like performing the ceremony here. He's a good man."

"Good." I told Grandma about the beautiful floor now that the Two Jims were finished. We agreed to do the final cleaning ourselves. The phone rang and it was Aaron.

"Grandma, I'm grabbing a bottle of wine and going over to Aaron's. Go ahead and eat without me." I went downstairs to the wine cellar. Another reason I hated fetching the bottle was because I had to punch in numbers to unlock the door. Guess it was Grandpa's way to stifle teenage drinking and he's never removed the lock. When downstairs, I'd always hear strange noises and jump, only to realize it was the furnace kicking on or the motor in the wine cellar, which kept it at an even temperature. Since Grandpa had once been a wine salesman and had also owned a wine store, "The Grapes of Craft," we were never in short supply.

Grandpa sat by the kitchen table when I returned to the room. "Hi, Grandpa." I gave him a kiss. "I'm spending the evening with Aaron."

"How's the floor?"

"Perfect. It's gorgeous. Grandma and I are going to finish cleaning up. There's dust from here to China and back." I still shivered from the basement dampness. "I'm going to talk to Aaron about having the wedding here. What do you say about that?"

"Anything for my granddaughter." Grandpa's eyes twinkled. "As long as I can walk the bride down the aisle, it doesn't matter where it's at."

"Thanks, Grandpa." I kissed both of my grandparents' cheeks. With the historic houses magazine and the bottle in hand, I headed out the door. A couple minutes later I was at Aaron's back door, where he greeted me with a kiss.

"Missed you."

"You too."

I tossed the magazine down on the table.

"Before we start talking about the picture, I have to ask—do you really want a church wedding or can we get married at my house?" I held my breath, waiting for his answer.

"It doesn't matter. I just want you."

"Good." I let out my breath. "I hoped you'd say that."

"What's on your mind?"

"There are too many coincidences. I also have something to tell you, but I've been afraid to."

Aaron held the corkscrew in one hand, the bottle in his other, and stared at me. "Tell me. Just because I'm a cop, you shouldn't hold anything back. We have to trust each other, honey," he said opening the bottle.

"I know. I'm just afraid of further questioning or suspicions." I watched him pour the glasses. My heart thumped because of his silence. I took the offered glass. "Thanks, dear."

"You don't need to worry, honey. They know you didn't kill her. They've told me." He leaned over and kissed me. "You've got to trust me," he said.

"I do." I took a swallow and started for the living room, and he followed.

"What's on your mind?" Aaron asked.

"I'm wondering about that burglar. That person who tried to steal the cufflinks? Did you do any investigating into the matter?" I asked, twirling my glass of wine. "I think Grandpa hid them because of their value, and the burglary from a long time ago."

"August was right. The burglar is dead and, by all reports, he had acted alone. It was during the Great Depression when no one had extra cash," Aaron said, shrugging. "Everyone was broke. Everyone needed cash. Brother can you spare a dime?"

"How true," I agreed. "They're in the birdcage drawer up in the attic." I sipped from my glass. "Pretty smart, eh?"

"Not bad." He pursed his lips. "Have the detectives questioned you about the dolls?"

"Surprisingly, no they haven't."

"They've had their hands full with questioning suspects. There's been no real leads, at least from what I can tell. I bet they'll soon be in contact."

"I'm sure that you're right," I said, raising the wine to my lips.

"Tell me your first thoughts when you saw the sampler picture from the Hamilton house."

"Really weird. It made my hair stand on end! But think about it. Now we have two roses. Dolley bequeathed the cufflinks upon her death to Elijah Putnam. who was distantly related to Grandpa and me." I set my empty glass down.

"Tell me that this isn't all a coincidence or not meant to happen. I believe it was all going to happen," Aaron said.

"Let me do a quick search on Polly." I reached for Aaron's iPad and came up with a few sites. "You won't believe this."

"She had a bird named Polly?" Aaron's eyes opened wide.

"Let's get a sheet of paper to draw the two samplers. It'll give us a better perspective." I went to his computer printer and removed a few blank sheets. I reached for a stray pen. "I'll start with Grandma's. Go and get the magazine from the kitchen table, will you?" He walked out as I began to draw. I knew the design and dates like the back of my hand, and had it on paper almost instantly.

"Here." Aaron set the open magazine page down in front of me. "We need a magnifier."

As he went to find one, I began drawing the second sampler, beginning with the larger embroidered motifs. With the magnifier, I counted the dots on the strawberry sidebars. The center dates were identical to the dates on Grandma's sampler. Puzzled, I sat back and studied the two drawings after I'd finished. *The samplers were filled with clues.*

"What do you think?" Aaron scratched his head as he reached for the paper. "I believe that clues abound, we just have to figure out their meanings."

"Polly means something. I bet it's where she buried it. Whatever 'it' is."

"Yes, whatever 'it' is that we're looking for, but it's been over two hundred years!" Aaron rubbed his jaw. "It doesn't fit."

"We have to keep digging. Are there two more samplers out there—somewhere?" With shaky fingers, I took the paper from him and held it up to the light. "Thirteen dots on each strawberry. Thirteen strawberries, top and bottom. Four along the sides. All are going up and down as if dancing. What does that mean when the top and bottom are aligned?"

"They are almost identical." Aaron stared at the paper. "We should make a list of all these coincidences. Maybe we can see a pattern?" He got up and pulled out another blank sheet, and sat back down. "Where should we begin?"

"We'll start with the murder. That has to tie-in here, somehow." I studied the drawn picture. "I know the answer is here, but where? What is it?"

"Right. Good as any place to begin." He wrote *Jackie Newell's Murder* at the top of the page. "Why did she come to Minneapolis? Why to your store? There must be plenty of dollhouse stores across the country or world, right?"

"It's because of the lineage connection." I sat back and thought hard, clicking reasons off on my fingers. "Number one, the White House. No other doll store specializes in these eras, the early White House years—whatever you want to call it." When Aaron raised his brow, I said, "It comes down to the dolls. I swear it."

"What about the dolls?"

"It can't be the dolls themselves. Something about the dolls, like the cufflinks. But—why kill for them? Who would know that she was going to see me?" I thought about the many orders of dollhouses that I've made in the past few years, which includes the dolls. Sewing all the Inaugural gowns is no easy feat especially when they have to be as close to perfect as possible. Learning to package all the furnishings and have them delivered without breakage wasn't easy. The first shipment of the Kennedy White House I had found tricky because the flowers are fragile. I placed each individually in a plastic bag and blew air around them so they wouldn't break, and it worked. "I wonder about the samplers?"

"But how can they be connected to the cufflinks?" Aaron stared at me, tapping the pen on the table.

"The White House, male clothing, that's what stands out." He starred the two entries. "It seems as if she was after the cufflinks, but why?" He threw down the pen. "What are we missing?"

"How it ties in with the samplers. How Grandma's and the one shown from Hamilton's house in the magazine are so similar, but have different corner motifs. What's the connection and what or why does it have my curiosity? There's something that I'm not seeing."

"As in what are we missing? A sign?" Aaron asked.

"Also, the gadroon and Polly are puzzling. Would she have buried the bird?" I asked. "I believe that once we figure out the meaning behind each corner and the dancing strawberries, we'll have a clearer picture of what we're after."

"What's the significance of the rose?" Aaron asked.

"It's symbolic. Roses are a symbol of love and romance." I chuckled. "I get it. The rose depicts James or Jemmy, as she called him. Jemmy was her love. They were lovers!" I grinned. "Can it be that simple? Or is it that we're after a greatly loved item?"

"Hard to say." Aaron leaned over and kissed my ear, then gave me tiny kisses down my throat. "What do you think?"

"Honey." My cell phone interrupted our foreplay. "Just a minute, let me shut this off." I reached for it, and found that I'd just received a new message. I opened it. It read: times up. I dropped the phone. Fear zipped through my body. I jumped up and wiped my sweaty palms on my jeans. "Look." My voice was so shaky I barely recognized it. "It's them."

Aaron read the message. "We're turning this over to the detectives."

"I'll call right now." I reached for the phone. I spoke directly to Detective Erlandsen. "I'm at Aaron Reynolds' house. I'll be at my house in five."

"Who is this from?" Aaron held up the envelope that had fallen from my purse.

"I don't know. Forgot about it." I put the phone back into my bag. "Open it."

I shivered as my shaky fingers ripped open the envelope and held up the stark paper with only one word printed in capital letters.

"Beware," I said. My voice cracked when I handed it over to Aaron. "They've got to see this too. I'm scared."

"I'm sticking it in a plastic bag. Hold on, we'll walk over together."

I told myself to calm down as I tried to make sense of the situation, until his return. He encircled me in his arms and whispered, "It'll be all right."

"Maybe I should go up to the attic and get the cufflinks."

"August and Marie should be in on this too." He stared into my eyes. "It's the right thing to do. They need to know."

"I know."

About the same time that we entered the kitchen, the detectives were pounding on the front door. Grandpa answered it as Aaron and I walked into the living room. Grandma gave us a concerned look as she stood up and came toward us. She gave me a big hug and we watched Grandpa let the detectives in.

"Detective Mergens, sir." He showed his badge.

"Detective Erlandsen, sir." He showed his badge. "I believe that Liv Anderson is here?" He peered around Grandpa, who'd stepped aside.

"Right over here." Grandpa nodded toward us. "Liv?"

"Right here."

"About the phone message?" Detective Erlandsen asked, reaching for his pad and pencil.

"Yes. It says, 'times up'. How did they get my number? It's private."

"Let me see it," Detective Mergens said, holding out his hand. He flipped it open and pressed a few buttons. "I'd like to keep this for evidence." He slipped it into his pocket.

"I also just found this letter and opened it. It came in yesterday's mail. It's ominous, also." I glanced around the room. "It says, 'Beware'."

"Let me take it and we'll have it analyzed." Erlandsen reached out for it. He placed the plastic bagged envelope into his inside pocket. "Go on."

"This is terrible. Can't you do something? Her life's in danger!" Grandpa said.

"I want to hear how you got the dolls." Erlandsen said.

"I admit it. I stole them from the bar. They were on the table. Stone had been looking at them."

"You should be charged for theft, ma'am," Detective Erlandsen stated. "This case hasn't made any sense from the start, so for now, you're off the hook. It was in a public place." He stared at me. "Don't ever let me hear of you doing something like this again!"

"I won't! I promise."

"Where are the dolls and the cufflinks?"

"Up in the attic."

"I'll join you." Mergens followed me to the stairs.

Upstairs, I pointed upward to the attic hatch. "Hold on, I have to get something to step on." I returned immediately with the stool in hand, set it underneath the hatch, and climbed up, opening the entrance and pulling down the steps. "Be right back."

"What's all up there?"

I turned back to glance down at him. "All kinds of old, old stuff. You wouldn't believe it. The cufflinks are in an old birdcage."

"My grandma never had an attic." He began climbing up the steps, and he popped his head into the hole. "Lots of stuff." He glanced around the room. "Bunch of antiques and boxes. Who else knows about the attic?"

"Childhood playmates, not really sure who else." I showed him the dolls and cufflinks.

"Okay. Now get the cufflinks in a safety deposit box tomorrow, and I'm taking the dolls."

"Yes, sir."

## Chapter Eleven

From the detectives, we learned there wasn't enough substantial evidence to hold Wanda and Stone. They were free to go. The chauffeur's name for certain was Brad Bushfield, and his alibi checked out. His address was in Minneapolis, and his spouse was Dorrie. The fact is, this made me uneasy for some reason. What had Brad heard as Jackie's chauffeur? Had he heard talk about the secret cufflinks or the family secret? I had to keep Dorrie close.

Aaron and I hadn't discussed Dorrie as a suspect since she was a childhood friend. I couldn't think of Dorrie as wanting to cause me harm, but what about her husband? I didn't know him. Were they short of cash? She had talked about the sampler, and she'd been in the attic, but it was years ago. I wasn't sure if I'd sleep again until the murderer was caught.

"I'm scared. Now that they're free, what's to become of the investigation?" I sipped my soda and set the glass down on the table.

"The detectives go back to square one. That's to find the motive." Aaron waited before continuing, "Don't worry. They'll find the killer. Everything will work out in the end. Nothing more will happen to you."

"That warms the cockles of my heart. You don't know for certain. The killer could be watching us through binoculars right now." I stared at him. "What about Dorrie? How is that she never told us she was married until recently plus the relationship between Brad and Jackie? She's got to be up to something. Brad had to have heard something while chauffeuring Jackie around."

"Livvie, calm down, honey. Dorrie's a grown woman. She's not a suspect. You've got too vivid of an imagination, or else you watch too many TV shows." Grandma sipped her root beer. "You're safe with us." She reached for my leg and gave me a love pat. "You're a sweet girl."

"Thank you, Grandma." I felt a little better, but not by much.

"I want the Madison dolls in my possession, and the cufflinks in the bank. I feel in my gut that the stolen museum jewelry is tied together. I'm beginning to wonder if the sampler isn't tied in with the secret, too."

"You could be right, Liv. It's one coincidence after another," Aaron said.

"How could the sampler be involved?" Grandma asked.

"We found an image of another sampler just like it in a photograph from the Hamilton House Museum," I said. "I've kept it between Aaron and me because it's so perplexing. This is all a huge puzzle."

"Really? How interesting," Grandma said. "Tell me about it."

"One different corner has a rose, the other three are like yours but without the flag. Odd, right?" I said.

"I should say so," Grandma said, slightly confused. "Let's get the cufflinks secured in the morning. It's best that way, August."

"You're right."

"Thank you." I noticed a car parking across the street and watched as Ronnie climbed from the car. He headed for his mother's house. Hazel lived kitty-corner from us, and I wondered if Ronnie wasn't picking his daughter up after her piano lesson. Hazel was a piano teacher. "Ronnie's at his mom's."

"Must be picking up his daughter," Grandpa said.

"You're right. There he goes." I sighed when Ronnie jumped into his car and sped away. "I worried that he'd want pictures." I rubbed my forehead. "I'd really like to plan my wedding, and not have to deal with a murder investigation. I'm staying home tomorrow. It's Saturday and wouldn't be busy. I can't help it. I'm going to plan my wedding and do some other investigations. I may just as well take off a few hours."

"Soon, the killer will be behind bars. Then you won't have to worry so much," Aaron tried to reassure me.

"I think I'm just going to go to bed." I finished my soda. "I'm giving Max a buzz to see if he can look after the store for me tomorrow. He should be able to handle the customers."

"Honey, I'm right behind." Aaron followed me into the kitchen. "Don't worry."

"Thanks."

Max said he'd look after the store for me plus catch the phone calls. He would work on carving heads and Grandpa would also be at the store to help out. Grandma had errands to run for the wedding. I decided to wait to contact Dorrie. I wasn't sure what to think about her, period.

I went to bed right away, burying my head under the blankets and staying there until eleven the following morning.

The house was quiet. I checked Grandma's phone for messages and learned Aaron had been called to work.

After getting dressed and slipping into a pair of jogging shoes, I stuck a water bottle into a belt pocket, and shrugged into an insulated jacket. A run down to Minnehaha Falls and back sounded good, even though the air was brisk and the sidewalks weren't completely cleared. I needed the fresh air to clear my mind, while the run gave me time to think.

I locked the doors behind me and headed toward the River Road, turned onto the Parkway, and followed it up to the park. The two-mile run left me thirsty. I took a drink from my water bottle near the creek bed where a statue of Hiawatha carrying Minnehaha across the rushing waters stood. The picnic area was void of the summertime crowds, which left me longing for longer, warmer days and nights.

Back home, I poured a glass of juice and ate two pieces of toast. Then I went upstairs to change. I glanced inside my grandparents' bedroom. Someone had turned the room completely topsy-turvy. My grandparents' jewelry was strewn across the bed, and dresser drawers were tipped upside down, toppled on the floor. Clothes, heaped in a haphazardly fashion, were spread all over.

I backed out of the room, rushed down the stairs, and plunked into the office desk chair. I quickly called emergency services before calling Aaron. Whispering, I said, "Help." I gave them my address and was told that the officers were on their way. *Who did this? Why? Am I alone in the house? What on earth were they after? Did this have something to do with the family secret?* My thoughts kept churning over and over. I eventually heard a siren. It became louder and then stopped outside our house.

"This way, officers," I said, opening the front door.

"You called it in?"

"Yes. Olivia Anderson. It's upstairs."

"Yes, ma'am. Have you touched anything?"

"I don't think so." I shook my head. "I think I backed out."

"Okay. Lead the way."

More uniformed officers entered. "We'll start canvassing."

"Up here." I had my foot on the bottom step when the two detectives arrived.

"Go ahead, officer," Erlandsen said.

"We're going to have a look around down here, then be up."

I continued climbing the stairs, and stopped outside of the room. "There it is. A huge mess. How awful. Why?"

"Ma'am? Any idea who would do this?" an officer asked.

"No, this can't be happening. It's Grandma's jewelry. I'll send her text, but I'm sure they'll return soon."

"You do that." He waited a beat, then said, "Downstairs."

"Yes." I took that as my cue to leave and headed back down the stairs only to see Aaron in the living room with the detectives conferring by themselves in another corner. "Aaron." I went to stand over next to him.

"I called August."

"Thanks."

Detectives Erlandson and Mergens asked the same basic questions the officers had, only in a different way. I was asked the same two questions in five different ways—Who? Why?

"Liv." Mergens cleared his throat. "Do you think this incident is connected to the murder? I'd like to know your thoughts."

"It's possible." I stepped away from Aaron.

"Olivia. Aaron." Grandma rushed into the living room and pulled me into her arms. "My goodness! What on earth is going on around here?" She released me, planted her hands on her hips, and pointed her finger at the detectives. "Will you please do your job and find the killer?" She jutted her chin out and glared at them.

I wanted to rein her in, but decided that the two detectives needed a tongue lashing.

"And furthermore—."

Grandpa charged into the room and joined the party. Aaron and I stepped to the side to watch the scene unfold.

"Grandpa." I gave him a stern look.

"Listen, detective. First my granddaughter has the store broken into, then murder. And now the killer is free to murder someone." Grandpa glared at him. "Don't look so shocked, Detective. Your department allowed this to happen."

"My husband is just trying to say, that you two best get off your duff and find the killer." Grandma pointed her finger right into Detective Mergens chest.

"Yes, ma'am." Mergens painted on a smile.

"Grandma. Grandpa. They're only following protocol." I waited a beat before continuing, "It's their job to find out what happened. Give them a break." I went to stand between Grandma and Grandpa, and held their hands. "I love you both, but please just back down."

"For now," Grandpa squeezed my hand.

"Only for the moment, honey." Grandma dried her eyes.

"Okay, then." I looked at the detectives. "It's like this. I went for a run, came home, ate, and then went upstairs to change. Notice something? I haven't changed." I motioned to my clothes. "See? I glanced into the room, and noticed the mess. That's when I called, after running into the office to use the phone."

"Got it all down." Erlandsen skimmed his notes. "We'd like an inventoried list of the missing items."

"Will do."

"We haven't seen the room yet, sonny. Remember?" Grandma had her hands on her hips and looked ready to start another avalanche of spitfire verbiage.

"Let's go up and take a look right now." I looked at Detective Erlandsen, who nodded. I wove my arm through Grandma's, and Grandpa followed us up the stairs. We stood at the door to peer in while the uniformed officer was stationed right inside of the door.

"How awful." Grandma gasped, clutching her chest. Tears streamed down her cheeks. "Olivia? Who would do this? Why would they want to hurt us?" She collapsed in Grandpa's arms.

"That's okay, Grandma. It's not you. They're after the cufflinks and the dolls."

"Aaron will find out who did this." Grandpa held Grandma tight against his chest. "We'll get through this."

"Officer?" I looked at him. "How long are you staying?"

"Till I'm told I can go."

Dumb question, I thought to myself as I ushered my grandparents down to the office where we found Aaron.

"The detectives went outside, but they'll soon be back."

I glanced at the corner of the desk where the rose was embedded, and Aaron nodded.

"Wait," Aaron mouthed.

The detectives reentered the house, heading into the office.

"Call anytime if you remember anything. It doesn't matter how minimal you think it is. Let us be the judge," Mergens stated.

"Here, take this," Erlandsen said as he handed me his card.

"Okay. Yours, I didn't have." I slipped the card into my pocket. "Anything else?"

111

"What about prints from the envelope and note?"

"Part of an ongoing investigation, ma'am." Mergens called up the stairs, "You can leave now."

"Okay," the officer responded. He came down the stairs and went out the door to the squad car.

"I think a shot of scotch is in order. All the way around." Grandpa got up and went over to the large globe, then pulled back the ring. It opened to his fresh stock of liquor.

"I don't care for one. I need some ice water." I said.

"I'm going back to work." Aaron kissed me, and left.

"We have to figure out a motive," I heard myself speak. "That's at the core of this investigation, and we don't know of any." I closed my eyes, opening them when Grandma returned with my water and a glass for herself.

"We believe, Aaron and I, that the cufflinks might be the core of the puzzle. We already know they were passed down through the ages and how you came to have them. I wish Aaron was here." I wasn't sure if I should continue or not. "Did you take the cufflinks to the bank, Grandpa?"

"No. They're safe. I had to help in your store, remember?" Grandpa said. "I will."

"Did you pick up the box of letters from the attorney today, Grandma?"

"No. It's been so hectic around here between your wedding and all that at the store. Besides, how on earth can a murder, which happened almost two hundred years later, be connected to the Madisons? It isn't possible," Grandma said, shaking her head.

"But, you see? That's what we don't understand." I sighed. "Grandma, have you ever heard of another sampler that's similar to yours?"

"No." She shook her head.

"Well, neither had I until we found that one in the Hamilton house. Awfully coincidental, don't you think?"

# Chapter Twelve

Because my grandparents slept in my bed that evening, I spent the night at Aaron's. We set aside Sunday to straighten up their bedroom.

Still shaken from the previous days' events, I had Maggie pick me up for our excursion to shop for wedding accessories along with her bridesmaid dress. Maggie's brown eyes sparkled, and rosy cheeks brightened my spirits and calmed my fears when I climbed into her small car.

A ring of suburbs surrounded Minneapolis and St. Paul. One of them, Bloomington, was the home of the Mall of America. We decided to make a quick stop there to look at wedding gowns and dresses. The two of us hadn't been out together in eons, ever since I got the brilliant idea to open my business. The morning sunshine felt wonderful, causing me to put on my sunglasses to fend off the snow's glare. The Mall's parking lots were filling up with holiday shoppers, but we were lucky at finding a spot. After parking, we hustled inside.

"Let's get a coffee first and watch all the good looking guys go by," Maggie gushed. She'd just split with her boyfriend of two years, and I felt sorry for her.

"Double shots." We hiked to the nearest coffee shop and ordered.

"Should we buy my dress today, or what's your plan?" Maggie took a sip of her coffee as we located a small table nearby.

"If we find something, then we buy. No time to lose, you know."

"What color?"

"I'd like red and white cuffs. Something like the gowns from the old movie, White Christmas, with Bing Crosby and Danny Kaye." I caught her looking at some fantastic man who was strolling by. "The colors will go great with your dark hair."

"There's so darn many stores. Let's just drink up and hit the nearest, and then go someplace else."

"I'm in agreement." Maggie picked up her cup and started walking away, with me right beside her.

"Why do you think Dorrie never told us about her marriage?" We stopped a moment. "Why keep it secret?"

"Geez. I really can't say. Dorrie was always jealous of you. She'd always try to wear similar clothes and do her hair the same way as you, remember? She always wanted to be seen and maybe her jealousy holds through today."

"How so?"

"Aaron's a police officer and her husband's a chauffeur. That might upset her."

"It shouldn't, but it makes you kinda wonder, doesn't it?" We kept hiking briskly around the perimeter of the mall until finally we slowed to a normal walking pace. The bridal shop was around the corner, and we entered. After Maggie tried on three dresses, we decided to look elsewhere because they didn't fit properly. We drove to an independently owned store in Edina, another nearby suburb. The owner, Debbie, showed us a beautiful short-length, empire-waist dress, which fit Maggie nicely. Debbie, who was also a seamstress, fitted my mother's wedding dress for me next. Since I was shorter than my mom, the hem needed re-stitching, and our bust lines were slightly different, so an extra tuck was needed before the big day. Fortunately the dress didn't have many pleats for ironing. The dress accentuated my cleavage, which I liked, and slimmed my figure. Little else needed to be done as the dress had been well-cared for over the years.

Debbie wrote up a receipt, and we were ready to leave.

"We'll return in a week," I told her.

"Both dresses will be ready."

Maggie and I walked out.

"What about shoes?" Maggie glanced at me as we climbed into the car. "Should we go looking?" She started the car's engine then drove out of the parking lot.

"Let's have lunch first—it's on me."

We both loved Italian, so Maggie entered the freeway and headed toward the nearest chain restaurant. The afternoon went fast. I also purchased matching satin shoes with three-inch heels.

"Now, we're set." I grinned, happy that my mother's dress worked. I hoped she would be proud of me since I chose to wear her dress for my big day. As Maggie parked in the driveway behind my grandparents' house, I thought of the many years that we'd known each other.

"Remember when we'd play dress up?" I thought of the old dresses that Grandma hauled out of the attic for us to play in.

"Those huge hats. They almost swallowed us up. Don't forget the one with the bird on it. It looked so real."

"Oh, wow. Memories." I climbed out of the car and leaned into the window. "Catch ya later." I moved away so she could backup.

"Yep."

With my bag in hand, I walked over to Aaron's only to find the door locked. I thought he'd be home, and then remembered that he had errands to run. I crossed the lawn and went into the kitchen, where I found two notes from Grandma.

*What would you like for supper?*

*A. Grilled Norwegian salmon and veggies*

*B. Beef roast*

*C. Nothing because you won't be here*

I circled *C*, because I felt sure that I would spend time with Aaron. I still didn't know where Grandma was. She had a way of keeping to herself when she wanted to. The other note read:

*How did it go today?*
*Would you like me to be your bodyguard tomorrow?*
    *Yes*
    *No*

I circled *Yes*, since it probably was a good idea to have a bodyguard. We also needed to take care of the mess in the bedroom. It was already four o'clock, and I was home alone. I reached for my phone and gave Aaron a call. It was decided that we'd have dinner with his best man, Tim, another police officer.

I peeked into Grandma's room and saw that the drawers were replaced, the clothing picked up. *Why didn't Grandma put away the jewelry?* I thought about the hat that Maggie had mentioned. *What kind of bird was on that hat?* I decided to go up into the attic and try to find it. I brought the stool over to the area under the ceiling hatch, climbed up, and released the hatch. The steps dropped down, making it ready for me to climb up into the attic. I turned on the light.

I got the jitters as I stood looking around. I couldn't shake the feeling that someone else had been up here, but everything appeared normal. Nothing looked disturbed. I brushed my sweaty palms against my pants and reached for the large hatboxes. The top box lid was hard to remove because it was so dried out. I grinned as I pulled out the hat. It looked like a flower garden. I replaced the lid and opened the box directly below the first, and that hat featured long, narrow peacock feathers. The hat in the final box had the brim with the bird on it. Inside the lid lip, there was a short note: *"Thank you for the strawberry ice cream recipe."*

What in the world? I searched the hat for more writing but found little else. The bird was a parakeet. *Back to the bird and strawberries again.* I scratched my head before placing the hat back in the box and replaced the lid. I carefully looked at the other hats once again, but they were void of writing. The dates on the boxes were worn off. Next, I went to the birdcage to make sure that the possessions were still safe. I groaned when I saw the cufflinks because they were supposed to be brought to the bank for safekeeping. Since the bank was closed, I left them but made sure that I hadn't brushed the dust away. I climbed out of the attic and closed the hatch cover.

After showering, I decided to wait before dressing because I didn't want to wrinkle my dress. Instead, I put on a robe, went downstairs to the office, and fired up the computer. As I waited, my grandparents returned.

"In here," I called. I logged into the store's e-mail and began responding to the messages—all thirty-six. I deleted several messages asking how I killed Jackie, which caused me to fume. A few reporters wanted interviews. I glanced at the doorway when I heard my grandparents approaching. Grandma was holding an extra glass of wine, and Grandpa had a bottle in his spare hand.

"Just what I needed." I took a sip. "Thanks."

They sat down together on the settee. "The showroom looks really good." Grandpa placed his arm across Grandma's shoulder to kiss her cheek. "It's like brand new."

"Monday, we'll clean the shelves. Dorrie asked to help. The three of us will get it done in a minute." Grandma sipped. "Tell me about shopping."

*I'm keeping Dorrie right by my side and asking about her marriage.*

"That's okay, dear," Grandma said. "Your parents would be so proud and happy with your choice. Aaron's a good man."

"Thank you." I smiled.

"What are you looking up?" Grandpa refilled our glasses. I was happy to have a change of subject.

"Polly was the name of a bird, right?" I started thinking about that hat. "Maggie remembered us playing dress up while wearing that huge hat with the bird. Don't you think it's a little coincidental?"

"What are you getting at?" Grandma set her glass on the table. "Someone was murdered for a bird? It doesn't make sense." She shook her head.

"I know. I'm really perplexed." I glanced at the clock and, at the same time, Aaron entered the room. "Hi. We're having a family discussion about a bird."

"A continuation?" He reached for the empty bottle, frowning. "How soon will you be ready?"

"Fifteen. Is my little black dress in order?" I noticed Grandpa's ears turned red while Grandma blushed. "Log me out." I got up.

"That's only to wear for me. Wear your navy one instead." He smiled and gave me a kiss as I walked past him. He crawled in behind the desk to sit down.

In the bathroom, I brushed out my hair and pulled it back into a curly ponytail, leaving ringlets framing my face. I applied red lipstick, and put on sparkly red earrings to match. The navy dress slipped on easily. I blushed, knowing where his hot palm would leave its mark.

After saying good night and giving my grandparents each a kiss, we left. We decided we'd meet at the local Chinese Dragon restaurant, where they served wonderful eggrolls and chicken chow mein.

Tim and his date, Peggy, arrived right on time.

During dinner, Peggy had the audacity to ask about the murder and who did it.

"I didn't, that's for sure, and so far there's no firm suspects." We quickly ate and left.

"Let's run by the store and take a look at the floors," I said in the car as we crossed over the 694 bridge, heading toward downtown. We were getting near the exit for the dollhouse store, and I was anxious to see the floors. "Let's go in and dance before we fill it with the dollhouses."

"It's not a dancehall, and it might scratch the wood." Aaron made the turn for Main Street. "But, it would be fun."

"That's my man." I smiled, and clutched his hand. "Do you still want Tim in the wedding?" I liked Tim, but wished that Peggy hadn't been so rude.

"I bet he'll message me before long. He'll have it all figured out. Trust me." He slowed as we drove past the front of the building.

"Did you see that?" I gasped.

"See what?"

"Park right over there." I pointed to an empty spot three cars down from the front of the showroom windows. "Look! I could swear I saw a light."

"Not possible. We shut off all the lights and locked the doors. Besides, the alarm system would sound if someone entered," Aaron said.

We stared toward the windows and saw a light beam.

"You're right. There is a light."

"Of course. I'm not seeing things." I opened my car door to get out while at the same time Aaron grabbed my arm. "I want to see. Let me go."

"You're staying right here, honey, while I go check it out. I don't want anything to happen to you. If I see anything, I'll call for a squad car." He held my hand. "Trust me."

"Okay." I knew that I wouldn't stay, but it made him feel better.

Aaron got out and quietly closed the door, barely latching it. He reminded me of a movie character as he stole across the street. I waited until he was in the shadows, before doing the same. It wasn't long before I was standing beside him. I could tell by his not-so-friendly muttering, "Go back," that he wasn't too happy.

"Not on your life." I stood right beside him and didn't move unless he did. We inched closer to the windows. "Hurry up. It's cold out here."

"Quiet or go back to the car," he muttered over his shoulder.

I wanted to growl back but figured that I might press my luck. When we were in front of my door, I tried to calm my pounding heart. My sweaty palms itched, and I curled them inside my pocket. At the side of the window, we both saw the curtain of light trail across the shiny floor.

"Who is it?" Aaron had peeked from the bottom corner of the window.

I nudged his back when he didn't answer. "Well?"

"You won't believe this." He stood, and knocked.

I peered inside.

"Mikal?" I shook my head. Now I had an older man investigating on my behalf. I pressed in the code and opened the door, letting Aaron enter first. I turned on a light.

"You won't believe this, but I'd had an analysis party this evening, and started walking to my car with one of the ladies. We stopped for a minute in front of your store, she touched the knob. Presto! It opened." Mikal said.

"Busted is more like it." I stared at him. "Really. Why are you here?" We stood near the counter. "Let's go into the workroom where we can sit, shall we?"

Aaron led the way. I shut the light off in the showroom and turned one on in the workroom. We each found a chair and sat.

"That's exactly how it happened. I had had a handwriting party in my store and walked out with a guest. The woman, I think her name was, Alice, twisted her ankle, leaned against your door—and it popped open," Mikal said.

"I've never heard anything like this before," I said.

"It's all true," Mikal said.

"Go on. There's got to be more to it." Aaron glanced at me.

"Let me tell you about this underground cavern," Mikal said. "It's like a long basement."

"When were you down there last?" Aaron asked.

"I'm not sure if I've been down there more than once or twice, which was a very long time ago."

"It runs under this whole block?" Aaron said, his hands on his waist. "I don't believe it." He shook his head.

"It's got to be registered in the city records."

"What was the basement used for?" Aaron looked at Mikal.

"The corner restaurant was a speakeasy during Prohibition. I suspect that John Dillinger and Al Capone and the rest of the thugs may have used it as a hideaway, or for stashing liquor from the police." Mikal rubbed his chin. "There's a bathroom down there, too, don't forget. Should we go look? The door is hidden and the steps are treacherous."

"This whole thing is getting more and more bizarre." I scratched my head. "We have dolls stolen. Cufflinks. Birds. Roses.

Old embroidered samplers. And now Prohibition." I removed my ponytail and untangled my hair. "How do they relate?"

"The police have checked the hatch and saw that it's sealed. The hatch by the front door. There's that other back door which is hidden near ours. Since the police have knowledge of it, we should be allowed inside." Aaron raised his brow. "Should we?"

"Eew! It might be full of mice and bugs and spiders," I said. No way would I be left behind. "Lead the way."

"Follow me," Mikal said.

Aaron and I followed Mikal outside. The stairs were right outside the back door, hidden under the outside iron fire escape steps, which led upstairs to Max's. Which made me wonder where he was. It seemed strange that he hadn't joined us. Mikal shined the flashlight on the door, and we noticed that the magnetic strip from burglar alarm was compromised.

"This has to be called in and reported." Aaron looked at me. "Know anyone who would've gone down there?"

"Not at all."

"There are two doors. This one and the door at the other end." Mikal handed the flashlight to Aaron.

"The restaurant. See how the door's hidden by shrubs? That's why no one knows it's here."

"You two go back inside to wait. I'm staying right here."

"It's coming to a head." Mikal tried to lead me inside.

"I'm stayin' right here." I stomped one foot then the other on the ground as I crossed my arms. "And, that's final." I clamped my mouth shut and jutted out my jaw.

"You're impossible." Aaron glared at me while he dialed the police to speak to the dispatcher. He closed his phone, slipping it into his pocket. "They'll be here any minute."

"She's right, Aaron." I watched his brow twitch while Mikal talked. "What if someone, the killer, came and clubbed you on the head? She'd protect you."

"Good grief! The gorilla-man could return." When Aaron gave me a blank look, I explained, "The bodyguard or else the chauffeur.

They were both huge. By the way, why were they dropped from suspicion?"

"They, meaning all three including Wanda, had tight alibis." Aaron rubbed his chin.

"So what you're saying is that they alibied each other." I rubbed my temples. "They're not off the hook in my book."

## Chapter Thirteen

I sat in the workroom but could still heard sirens in the distance. When the back door squeaked open, I said, "In here."

"Livvie?" Mikal entered and touched my shoulder. He came around to face me. "This will soon end."

"How? How do you know?" I still didn't feel any closer to the answers.

"I just feel it. I'm psychic too." Mikal shrugged, then scratched his head.

"It all remains to be seen." I smiled when I realized that Mikal was serious.

"They'll be coming in soon." Mikal found a chair to sit on and glanced around the room. "It's no accident that I'm here."

"Why do you say that? I'd really like to know why you were here." I ran my fingers through my hair, glanced down at my dress, and then at my ring. "What a night. How many people were in that hand analysis party of yours?"

"Ten, but Alice hung around. This is all the truth, I swear to you." He rubbed his chin. "And here I am and look at what we found."

"I'll have to believe you. The police will get to the bottom of it all. I wonder if anything will materialize?" We turned as Aaron entered.

"I'll leave you two and we'll talk tomorrow." Mikal stood.

"Thank you." I waited until he walked out the door before looking at Aaron.

"Don't worry, baby. When things are at the worst, the end is near. The detective's and a two officers are inspecting the basement."

After a while I pulled back, just as the police entered.

"Ma'am," a uniformed policeman spoke, "ever seen this before?" He held a bagged earring up for me to see.

"Good grief. Yes, I have seen it," I said. "I think I know whose it is, Dorrie's. She was missing one the other day." My eyes opened wider and I gasped. "Why would her earring be lost there?"

"We don't think anything, ma'am." The officer looked at Aaron. "Got her name and number?"

"I believe it's all on file, but sure." Aaron glanced around the room. "Where's your bag?"

"In the car, remember?"

"Right."

"Her name is Dorrie Fillmore." I gave them Dorrie's telephone number. "I've wondered about her, and now the chauffeur, her husband, Brad. He could very likely have killed Jackie Newell after learning what's at stake for the family secret, which we don't know what it is."

"Thank you, ma'am." The officer closed his notepad. "We've searched down there and nothing seems amiss. We'll issue a full report in the morning."

"How'd they get in?"

"The person had put a piece of foil between the magnetic strip and the door for easy entrance." He gave me a half smile. "I'll see myself out."

We watched him leave.

"Let's go home."

Finally we left for home, and I spent the night with Aaron. I hated the idea of sleeping alone after a night like that.

The gray morning skies fit my mood, and I groaned as I rolled over and pulled the blanket up over my shoulders. Aaron woke me with a tray of bacon and eggs and a glass of orange juice. I knew I had to get busy. I expected a phone call from Grandma at any time, and I wasn't sure how to explain that Dorrie wouldn't be able to join us to clean up the store.

"Just say she had errands," Aaron mentioned. It was like he read my mind.

"How did you know I was thinking about that?" I sat up and worked on cleaning my plate. He sat beside me, and watched.

"Because you haven't called Marie, that is, Grandma. Normally you've touched base with her by now."

"Has she called?"

"Voice mail."

I finished my meal before removing Aaron's tray. I jumped into the shower and slipped on some old work clothes that I'd left behind, and then gave my hair a good brushing. When finished, I met him downstairs.

"I heard from Tim." Aaron told me.

"Yes?" I sat opposite him on a kitchen chair.

"He broke off with Peggy. I believe he will be attending the wedding alone. He asked me to give you his apologies. He will probably give them in person at a later date." Aaron frowned. "You're fine with that, aren't you? It was Peggy who was the rude one, not Tim."

"Sure, fine." I wanted to put the dinner out of my mind.

"You're beautiful."

"Thank you." I blushed from head to toe. "I was just going to call Grandma so that we can get started in the store cleaning it up to have it ready soon for business." I reached for the phone and dialed. "Hey, there. Did Aaron tell you about last night?" I didn't mention Dorrie's name or say anything about the earring, nor did she. We hung up deciding that we'd drive to the store separately, in case I wanted to stay late. I also wanted Mikal to do another handwriting analysis. It always soothed my mind.

After kissing Aaron goodbye, I headed out the door. As I walked the shoveled path to my car, I found Grandma standing by the garage door, waiting for me.

"Livvie, I can't move with your car sitting in front of mine."

"Yes, Grandma." I gave her a smooch before unlocking my car and jumping inside.

I hadn't noticed the sanding dust in the showroom last night, but now I thought about it, and wondered how bad it was, as I turned onto Cedar Avenue, heading toward downtown. Cedar angled up toward Washington Avenue. I passed under where there'd once been a railroad viaduct used by the Burlington-Northern and the Hiawatha lines. Before long, I turned onto Main Street. As I parked behind the building, Grandma parked right beside me. We got out of our cars at the same time.

"Should we get a 'cuppa joe' before going inside?" Grandma motioned toward the café where I usually picked up a cup.

"Good idea. It'll help us to think better." I winked.

As we returned to the store, I realized how nice it would be to reopen. The store looked like it was brand new. I opened the back door and followed Grandma inside.

Grandma coughed.

"We have a lot of dusting to do," I said as I locked the door behind us, and after dropping our belongings in the workroom, we walked straight ahead to the showroom. We stood in the center and stared upward. "We need a couple of dust mops."

"You're right about that." I glanced at the walls. "The walls need dusting, but the floor is in good shape."

While Grandma dusted the shelves, I went into the workroom to begin removing the picture coverings and wiping them. Grandpa arrived with dust mops a little while later.

"Everything going okay?" He asked with his hands on his hips. "Where's Grandma?"

"Out there." I nodded toward the showroom.

"Oh, sure." He headed out the door. I smiled when I heard, "It's about time you got here," from Grandma.

The day slipped by. I plugged in an old Bing Crosby CD for Grandma. I didn't want her leaving early because of the 'noise' coming from the radio. I started humming the words from 'Swinging on a Star'. I looked at Grandma and said, "I wish I could read the words on a screen."

"Just like Mitch Miller's bouncing ball." She grinned.

I chewed on what she'd said as we labored side by side. I thought of the DVD Mikal gave me with several of Mitch Miller's programs and decided to watch another as soon as possible. However, I wish I could've figured out what it was that tickled my brain. I gave up and thought about the night before.

My mind replayed the events. I wondered what was happening with Dorrie. I wondered what would come out of the questioning. I couldn't picture her as a killer, but how well do you really know a person? I thought of Jackie and how she didn't deserve to have her head smashed by a hammer, either. I shuddered while the image of her looped through my mind. As my thoughts went deeper, I recalled once again Jackie's question about a family secret. Why would she ask that?

My phone buzzed, yanking me from my thoughts. There was a voicemail from Dorrie saying that she was on her way to the store.

"Grandma? Dorrie will be here any minute. Care to stay and hear what she has to say?" Resting against the counter near the computer, I speed-dialed Aaron, and glanced at Grandma.

"I'm beat," she said. "I'm also leaving because we have an appointment with an attorney about that box from my cousin who passed away. I'm to get it, since she had no children and I'm listed as the next of kin. I guess she must not have known what to do with it."

"I guess it doesn't really matter. What's in the box? Do you know?" I asked.

"Not really. Mom wasn't much for old things, and my grandma passed away when I was young. My cousin lived out of state so we saw little of each other. I bet it's been thirty years, at least." Grandma took a few deep breaths. "I need a rest."

"Take a nap, Grandma. Thank you for helping me. See you at supper." I held the phone tight against my ear as I waited for Aaron to answer, and ended up leaving a voice message. I told him that Dorrie was arriving soon, gave the time, and asked him to come to the store. I placed the phone inside my pocket and listened to Grandma closing the back door.

At last alone, I felt the lingering creeps from the night before slither up my spine. I pulled two clean dustsheets from the box in the workroom and went out to the showroom. It didn't take long for the floor to shine. I was admiring the walls, ceiling, and floor, when I heard the back door open.

"In here!" I called, thinking it was Dorrie. I turned and saw that it was Max. "Where have you been?" I asked him.

"I had errands to run. Sorry." He cocked his head. "What's up?"

"A few things have been happening around here, lately." I crossed my arms and narrowed my eyes. "It's like this—someone broke into the doorway outside that leads to a rather large room under these three adjoining buildings. Have you seen anyone else lurking?"

"No, from what I can tell, there's been no one around besides a few of Mikal's customers. They leave and don't return." He gave me a serious look. "I've already been peppered by the police. I showed it to Dorrie because she asked about it. Then we came right back up. Didn't see any harm in it, because there's nothing down there."

"My goodness." I didn't know what to think anymore. "The cops don't waste time, do they?" I spun around, heading for the workroom. "I'm back here when Dorrie comes."

"Okay."

The back door opened and I heard Dorrie say something, and then saw her standing in the doorway.

"I quit." Her eyes were bloodshot, her complexion was clammy, and her voice weak. "I didn't kill anyone. Why did you call the police? Why not just ask me about the earring?" She burst into tears.

"Everyone's a suspect nowadays. The police are just doing their job." I stared at her. "I didn't know there'd be one of your earrings down there, Dorrie. This whole mess is driving me crazy. What did they ask?"

"The usual." She crossed her arms.

"There's been an awful lot going on around here." I stared at her. "It's time for true confessions. Why you didn't tell me that you'd married? We've been friends forever. Why keep it hidden? And now the earring down below. I'm not sure if I can trust you anymore."

"Brad said that if you ever found out who he was, you'd probably fire me."

"Really? Who is he?" I pointed my finger at her. "The truth. NOW!"

"It was his grandparents who killed your parents." She burst into tears. "Are you happy now that you know? I'm fired, aren't I?"

"His grandparents! You knew about it and didn't tell me?" I sank into the nearest chair. "I guess I don't really know you, do I?"

"I was trying to protect you."

"How did you know about the door?"

"I've always known it was there."

"How did you know that?" I studied her. Her story didn't seem to add up.

"My dad always talked about the speakeasies during Prohibition and Max mentioned this building was at one time."

"Now I know why you were interested."

Just then Aaron entered.

"Dorrie?" Aaron walked over to me, placing his arm on my shoulder. "I suspect that you're talking about the hidden door and secret passage."

"I'm sorry." Dorrie briskly walked from the room going straight out the back door.

"You know what I want to do?" I stood, snatched my phone, keys, and bag.

"Go for a walk." He stepped aside, motioning for me to pass. "I bet I know where too." He reached for the flashlight, which had been left from the night before. "We're ready."

"Let's go."

Aaron followed me over to the outside hidden door. After opening it, we climbed down the stairs in the shadowy daylight. At the base, he flicked on the flashlight. Straight ahead, the passage led us to the far end, opposite my building. To the side was one huge room. We saw a light bulb screwed into the ceiling in the center of the room with a pull string. Together we walked toward it. When Aaron pulled the string, the entire room lit up.

"It's almost like a dance floor." I slowly turned, gazing across the empty room to the far walls.

"It's like down here really doesn't exist. What a great hideaway."

"This building was built back in the late 1800s." I faced the far wall. "Let's walk the passage."

As we did, Aaron shined the light on each brick and cement crack. A couple places deserved further scrutiny, so he tried breaking or pulling away some bricks, but none of them moved. Candle sconces hung in three places, an odd brick pattern beside them.

"I wonder if the police noticed the pattern of these bricks change? Look at this." Aaron drew his finger down over the crack. "See that?"

"Wouldn't that have sprung open if it was a door?"

The overhead heating and cooling ducts hummed.

"Let's get out of here. I'm getting the creeps."

# Chapter Fourteen

I called the precinct to speak with the investigators and got Detective Erlandsen.

"This is Liv Anderson, and I'm calling about last night. Do you have the report?"

"It hasn't arrived yet. Wait a sec. My partner just handed it to me. I see someone entered but it was Mikal. The officers walked the length of that friggin' big room, but didn't find anything amiss."

"I think it needs further scrutiny."

"We'd already planned another friggin' walk through. We'll stop during our rounds."

When Erlandsen and Mergens arrived, they immediately went down the back stairs. Both asked me a million questions about the door and how it came to be opened. I told them about this morning along with Aaron and Mikal's discovery last night. After they left, I went to see Mikal before leaving for home.

Mikal was with a client, so I waited until he was free. When the woman stood and dug into her pockets for money, I got up and walked to the door. After she left, I went inside and sat down.

"Just a sec, Livvie." He looked at me over the rim of his glasses before reaching for his billfold to slip the cash inside. "I saw that the police are back. What happened now?"

"More twists and turns," I said. "You'll never guess what's happening now." I started to feel as if a weight was lifted from my shoulders. I took it for a good sign. "I think it is the beginning of the end."

"I knew it. Want a cola? It's on me." Mikal went to the vending machine, removed a bottle, then glanced at me. I nodded. It's really a joke, since the little vending machine is actually a refrigerator where he stores the food he brings from home. He handed me the can and sat. "Spill the beans."

"It's hard to believe that the door opened like that."

"It happened as I said." He took a drink. "Coincidences happen for a reason."

I took a drink and decided to Google search Mikal later. "Now for the big news," I said. "The police took a closer look at the duct work which eventually led them to exit at the restaurant."

"Oh my. This adds a whole new dimension. It means that the employees of the restaurant could've sneaked into the store, if they knew about it." Mikal's eyes grew wider, and he shook his head. "What do the police say?"

"They're pretty tight-lipped." I glanced at the clock. "Oops! Aaron's probably wondering about me." I stood up and said, "Catchya later." I walked right into Ronnie.

"What do you want?"

"The police were here last night and this morning. Why?" Ronnie asked.

"None of your business." I tried to brush past him, but he stepped in front of me.

"Play nice," Ronnie urged. "Remember that we're old friends."

I plunked my hands on my hips and glared at him. "Not on your life." Two squad cars parked. The detectives waved me over.

"We're taking a closer look at the basement," one said. "We're going to do a thorough search of the premises. You can operate your store. Do what you need to but stay out of the basement."

"Okay." I walked away, and went over to where Max stood.

"Have you told the police about being down there?" I cocked my head as I stared at him. "At least now I know the truth. I trust you, Max."

"I mentioned it during one of the many questioning sessions. It's recorded. What Dorrie said, I don't know. I wouldn't be privy to that."

"I'm glad that you told me."

"I'm sure it won't be much longer before they leave." Max put his arm over me. "Tell me what's happened. Why are there so many more cops? Just two would be all that's needed to walk through down there. Something else must've happened?"

"There's that duct system. The other opening goes up a set of stairs in the restaurant. There are weird cracks in the wall near the sconces."

"I wonder where this will lead?"

"We found an earring of Dorrie's." My eyebrows twitched. I wondered if I was onto something. "Have you told her anything?"

"Nope." Max scratched his chin. "I wouldn't ever say anything about our conversations."

"Hmm. I feel as if I'm getting closer." A trickle of fear raced up my spine as I pondered what he'd just told me. "Dorrie knows that Jackie was a descendant of Dolley, right?"

"Why do you ask?" He gave me a serious look. "Most of what we know stems back to Dolley, doesn't it?"

"Yes." That much I was certain about, and it was comforting to know that he agreed. Max was a good friend, and I wanted him on my side. "I have a theory but haven't come to any conclusions."

"Let's hear it, I'm all ears, as they say." His eyes twinkled. "I'm up for a good mystery." He picked up a tool, looked at it, then set it back down. "There's an awful lot of underlining bits that don't connect."

"You don't even know the half of it."

"Tell me. It helps to tell someone else sometimes."

"Did you know there's a sampler hanging in the Alexander Hamilton house almost identical to Grandma's sampler? It's chilling, really." I paused, giving him time to digest the news. "I think

Dolley hid something, and that's why Jackie asked me about a family secret. I think whoever killed her was privy to the information she knew, and they didn't want her to get what she was searching for. It's the usual motive, greed."

"Greed, money, propels most criminals, they say." He thought a moment before saying, "Okay. I didn't know that about Hamilton." He scratched his whiskers. "Continue. Not sure where this is going."

"Right. But. It's convoluted," I told him. "Before I continue, did you know that Dorrie and Brad the chauffeur, are married?"

"No."

"And, his grandparents hit my parents, and killed them. That's why she didn't tell anyone. Her excuse. I hope that's the end to her lies. It's been so many years since my parents passed away, that it seems odd to really speak of it."

"I'm sorry about that Liv, truly I am, but now tell me what else you were starting to. I'm tuned in."

"The killer either knew what the 'secret' was, or else he or she realized that there's something hidden and figured it would be worth a bundle. Brad picked them up at the airport, so he could've overheard their conversations right from the start. He had to have known about the cufflinks." I waited a moment to see if he'd say anything, but Max remained silent. "If it's not someone from Jackie's entourage, then it's someone close to me."

"Would anyone else know about the secret rumor besides the suspects? I know about August's cufflinks because I went to the anniversary. I remember seeing them and thought they must be expensive as hell. Selling them—you'd be set for life. I also know that the dolls tie in somehow."

"Oh. You do know. I should've realized that since we've been friends for so long." I took a deep breath. "It's unclear how many people know about the cufflinks. We've since found out that Dolley Madison had bequeathed them to an Elijah Putnam, who'd been a distant relative of Grandpa's. They also have a gadroon around them as do the cufflinks on Mr. Madison's doll. Grandpa's always kept them hidden and has only worn them a couple times." My heart pounded. "Did you mention the secret to Dorrie?"

"She was here when Jackie was, right?"

"No, but I'm sure she's heard us speak of it. She came in right after."

"Remember that old adage? Keep your friends close, but your enemies closer?"

"Sure. I think it was Honest Abe who said that. Why?"

"Find out what she knows." He studied me. "Those three wall sconces? Tell me again." Max shook his head and looked lost.

"Three cracked and patched-over places the size of narrow doors are right beside them."

"What next? This reminds me of one of those old detective movies from the thirties." He sighed. "What am I saying? Shit!"

"Exactly!" Sometimes he could be fun to be around. I stood up, and slipped into my jacket. "Let's see what else they've dug up."

We stood looking out the windows to watch as police came and went. Max opened the back door to have a smoke, and I decided to stand with him. Then I saw her.

"Max," I whispered. "Don't look, but I think I see Jackie's secretary, Wanda Brown." I stayed focused on her. "You have a better view than me. She's right under the street lamp, standing beside the man wearing that goofy, blue fishing cap. In fact, that man might be the bodyguard, Stone. It's hard to tell because of the brim shadowing his face. Take a picture."

"I'm on it." Slowly he removed his phone to snap a photo.

"What do you think? Is it or isn't it?"

"They're lookin' at us." Max slipped the phone inside his pocket. "Stay here." He moved away and mingled into the crowd.

I stayed next to the store while staying focused on the questionable couple, and noticed that the woman's height was about the same as I remembered Wanda's to be. The man's back and shoulders were gorilla-sized just like a weight-lifter's. I knew I was on the right track which propelled me to inch just a tiny bit closer.

"Honey, where are you?" Aaron called. I wanted to scream bloody murder, because the two people I'd been observing quickly disappeared.

"Shoot." I sucked in my breath only to blow it out long and hard. I wondered what happened to Max? He seemed to have disappeared, but then I heard his truck engine start. Just then, I heard Detective Mergens call my name. The detectives and I entered the store.

"Are you done?" I wanted them to go away.

"We found a few interesting things, but nothing substantial. Yes and no for the killer to use this as a hideaway. We're packing up now and leaving."

"Thank you."

"Anything else? Anything new to tell us?"

"Not that I can think of at the moment."

"For now, then. We'll be in touch."

"Yes." He walked out and I went into the workroom and removed my coat. Just then the backdoor opened once again and Aaron entered.

"The police will soon be out of here."

"I know. Thank you. I had to send away spectators." He left as my phone chirped. Instinctively, I knew it was Max. "I'll see you at home." Aaron left, and I immediately read the text message. 'im follow w n s'

*Oh wow! I thought. They're back. They're after the cufflinks!*

It was too late in the day. I sank into the chair, and stared straight ahead.

After a few minutes, I knew what I needed to do. I got up and went out to the computer, logging in. I punched in the county name. Links led me directly to the website for the original planning map of this area. After that, I searched for the records of the first builder plus the construction, the layout of the property, as well as adjoining buildings. It was as I expected. The underground unit ran from one end of the buildings to the other. Mine lay in the middle. Inga's antique store was beside the restaurant and Mikal. On my other side was another, smaller coffee shop. The diagram showed the trapdoors. Did they enter that way? I looked for hidden doorways, too, but didn't find any. I spent several more minutes searching the site, hoping for some kind of answers but that didn't happen. I got out of the site, and then clicked into Google. I started a search on samplers or embroidery. I wanted to learn as much as possible about the handwork, with hopes that I'd learn about the designs around the time of Dolley Madison.

The back door opened and I heard Max call, "They're staying at some sleazebag motel near campus."

"Did you get photos? Let me see them." Max retrieved the photos and displayed them on his screen.

"You don't look so good, Livvie. You're kind of green looking."

"Thanks." I peered closer at the images. It was a perfect shot of the two. "It's them. That's for sure. They're back because they want the cufflinks. They must need them in order to figure out the secret."

"I'm not sure what this is about, but your guess is as good as mine."

"Why a sleazebag motel?" I wondered out loud. "To stay incognito?"

"Sure. I wouldn't suspect that they'd hide there, would you?"

"No." I shook my head. "I'm calling the detectives."

"Good call."

I dialed the number, leaving a voice message on Detective Mergens's phone. Within minutes he returned my call.

"Liv? They can come and go as they please. We have no evidence to hold them."

"It's not right. It makes no sense for them to return nor does it to stay in a sleaze motel," I said.

"I agree with you, but they're off our radar for now."

"Thanks." I disconnected, fuming. "They're off the radar."

"Bloody hell," Max said.

"Exactly."

# Chapter Fifteen

Aaron and I sat together the following morning in Pastor Dahl's study. Pastor Dahl kept clicking his pen, an indication that he was very nervous. I couldn't concentrate because I wondered why the two killers were in town. I stared at the Bible verses in front of me.

"Which passage do you like best?" I asked Aaron, who seemed deep in thought.

"Let's go with *Genesis 24:48–51*."

"I want to walk down the aisle to the usual wedding march."

"Then it's settled." Pastor Dahl's brows arched. It made me think of a child's reaction to first reading out loud.

"My house is fine for the wedding?"

"Yes. I'd love it" Pastor Dahl said. He stood to shake our hand, and slightly smiled.

We bid each other good day. Aaron placed his arm over my shoulder when we set off.

"Why was he so nervous, I wonder?" We held hands until climbing into the car.

"There's been so much stuff happening lately, and hears all kinds of off-putting things. I'm sure he's on our side but quite worried about us," Aaron said.

"That's what it was." It finally dawned on me. "He's worried about the outcome of the investigation." I waited a beat. "He's known our family for a very long time."

"Yes, but he has to stay neutral. Parishioners probably call to ask a bunch of questions." Aaron drove away from the church.

"Any new leads?" I asked as we drove toward the store. He was going to help me get set up to reopen. "I'd like to know why those two are in town."

"It's not our business. They can come and go as they please." He frowned. "What's the plan for the store opening?"

"It's Christmas. Let's decorate for the holidays. I'd like to have hot cider, order White House Christmas cookies, plus have chocolate kisses." I looked at all the outside decorations as we drove toward downtown and turned up Washington Avenue. "Let's celebrate all the former First Ladies' December birthdays. I know Lady Bird Johnson was born in December, there must be other first ladies. Maybe Mary Lincoln. I'll have to check.

"First off, let's get the tables and houses set up. You two, meaning Max, can get started with that project. I'll call right away to place an ad in the paper. Afterwards, I'll begin gathering the furnishings for each house to take care of that end of the project," I said.

"We have our work cut out for us," Aaron said.

"Yes, through no fault of our own." I stared outside. "I don't understand what Jackie was doing in my store."

"She came to purchase houses, that's what we know for a fact or were made to believe." Aaron glanced at me. "Through speculation, it could be that she wanted a closer look at the remaining dolls. It could be that simple."

"This is true." I considered it a minute, then asked, "Why not just ask to see the other dolls? Why break in?"

"It's the secret."

"That's right. She wanted to know the secret and about the cufflinks." I pondered that a moment. "It stems from the samplers, but there has to be more to it than the samplers or the cufflinks."

"Whatever—maybe we'll never know." Aaron frowned.

"No. That's not an option." I shook my head. "I'm going to discover the family secret before the wrong person finds it. If Dolley did hide something, by golly, then it's worth the research and the discovery by someone who is honest. Not someone who has to lie, steal, and possibly murder to get it."

"I wonder what it is? What will you do with it, providing that you figure it out?"

"Hand it over to the proper authorities. Right where it belongs is where it'll go." I crossed my arms and enjoyed all the scenery as we drove. The light snowfall made the atmosphere romantic.

Traffic flowed easily. We turned across the Hennepin Avenue Bridge and headed for the store to park. "Let's get you set up."

"For sure. I hope Max has started already."

We walked to the door. Opening it, I heard Max in the showroom adjusting furniture.

"We're here," I called out.

"Good. I hope you brought Aaron."

I dumped my bag and coat in the workroom. I felt confident that whatever the killer was looking for, he didn't find it. The building was also secure. Nothing could possibly happen.

I walked with Aaron out to the showroom where we found several tables already standing. Max was adjusting another.

"Almost done." Max looked up at me, grinning. "Got up early. I'll carry down the two 1812 houses next."

"I can manage the ones from the workroom." Aaron gazed at the floor.

"Looks awesome. I don't see any blood stains." I smiled. "It looks brand new. I'm impressed, considering how dense the Two Jims acted."

"It's perfect."

I went back to the workroom to get started while they got busy arranging the display tables and houses. I called the newspaper to place an ad for the following Friday and Saturday. I also ordered several dozen cookies from a nearby bakery. I had purchased White House cookies from them before when I first opened the store so they had the appropriate cutters on hand.

Afterward, I began assembling the two dolls.

"Dolley, do you mind if I fit you in the empire waist dress? You're so beautiful in it, and I know that you make Mr. Madison jumpy when you wear it." I changed my mind about the Dolley gown, and decided to go with her red-velveteen empire waist dress with a royal ruby necklace. "What did you say?" I held her up to my ear to listen. "Oh! He chased you around the house the first time you wore it? How fun!" She was beautiful; James, very handsome. What a little man, I thought. He was the smallest president on record, five-feet, four-inches tall; weighing only 100 pounds. He also was the first president to wear trousers on a daily basis. I finished by pulling them up before slipping on his shoes. "Mr. President, give Dolley a running start, if you chase her. Okay?" I could swear that he nodded and winked his eye.

The morning chased by quickly. Aaron left shortly after moving the houses and setting them up. I gave Grandma a call to arrange for Grandpa to drop my car off at the store before they went to meet friends for dinner. Since Aaron needed to get some sleep, I would be on my own for the evening. His schedule dictated the graveyard shift; I always worried about him when he worked nights.

It took nearly all day to refurnish the two 1812 houses and have them ready for viewing the next day. Aaron placed the Andrew Jackson White House dollhouses on the table next to the 1812 pieces. I followed a timeline, when possible, because it helped prospective customers see how the White House evolved to its present day look. During Jackson's administration, the funds were appropriated to build the north portico. It covered the driveway to serve as a *porte cochere*, and put the finishing touch on the White House as we think of it today. Later, I planned to add the ground pieces, to make it seem a more time-honored display.

"There you are Mrs. Jackson," I said. I set her down in the bedroom. She died before his inauguration. A *divorcée*, she'd never been accepted into the social circles. I felt sorry for her because she lived her life as an invalid, it helped that Andrew Jackson was devoted to her.

It was almost five. I was about to give Grandma a buzz when Grandpa walked in to tell me that my car was here and that they were on their way to meet their friends. I grabbed my coat, bag, checked the front door, and the trapdoor twice to make sure they were locked. I decided to ask Grandpa to hire a carpenter to remove the trapdoor in order to put a new floor down in that section.

The nearest drive-through takeout joint was located on Lake Street, where I ordered a chicken sandwich, fries, and a soda before heading home. As I parked the car, I thought of beginning my research about samplers and embroidery. I also wondered if Montpelier had a similar sampler to Grandma's? It was worth looking into since the Hamilton House displayed one. I grabbed my bag, the food, locked the car doors, and headed up to the back door.

Once I entered the kitchen, I set the food down before removing my coat. I wondered if I shouldn't shovel the walkway, since a layer of snow covered it, but decided to sit and eat first.

The bird feeder outside the window was almost empty. I watched as a squirrel tried to get the last few seeds, and the spectacle made me grin. Watching squirrels was just as much fun as enjoying the beauty of the birds. I loved it.

After finishing my meal, I donned my jacket, boots, and headed out the door to scrape off the snow. It didn't take me long to clear the walkway. The footprints by the lower basement window did not catch my eye, at first. It was the messed up hydrangea bush in front of the window well. It was broken to pieces.

I put the shovel back in its storage place near the garage door before going over to take a closer look. I figured that damage had been done by a neighbor's cat or dog. Glass shards lay on the mulch surrounding the bush, but when I saw the entire window was busted out, my eyes opened wide. I called Aaron, who answered immediately.

"Just ready to fall asleep."

"The house was broken into."

"Be right there. Don't go in."

"I'm calling it in as soon as we disconnect," I said to Aaron. We immediately disconnected. Staring at the window well, I called

Detective Erlandsen's number. "Someone broke into the house. Aaron's here. I haven't gone inside since I noticed the broken window."

"Liv," Aaron called, briskly walking in slippers and wearing a T-shirt in below zero weather conditions.

"You didn't call 911?" Aaron yawned.

"I called you," I mouthed to him. I thought he looked ready to fall over in a heap.

"We'll be right there." Detective Erlandsen disconnected.

"That's why I called you first. This has got to be the work of Stone and Wanda."

"You can't jump to conclusions like that, Liv. It's dangerous especially without facts."

"Yes, dear," I groaned. I felt like biting him. I shrugged his arm off my shoulder. "This has got to end. I aim to get to the bottom of it. That's final."

"What about Marie and August? Called them, yet?" Aaron asked.

"Nope. I hate to do it. I feel so bad for them."

"That's okay. I'll do it. I hear the squad car coming, and they'll want to speak to you. Go ahead around front and bring them back here. I'll stay right here."

"Thanks." I hurried to the front, then motioned for the two officers to follow me to the backyard. Aaron stood in the same spot; when I appeared, he moved further away. "I was over there," I nodded toward the garage, "when I happened to glance this way. I thought it odd…" I waited while the officer wrote down what I'd said. "…for the bush to be stomped down."

"What time was that?"

"Just a few minutes ago. You see? Grandma's hydrangeas were trampled. That's when I went for a closer look. I stood right here. You can tell by the prints in the snow. I hadn't paid attention because of shoveling the deck when I first came home; I never looked over in that direction. I went right inside and ate."

By now, the snow near the window was a trampled mess.

"Thanks, ma'am." The two turned and stared at the broken window. "It sure looks like someone made their way inside. You didn't see anything different when you were inside, did you?"

"No. I never left the kitchen. I wouldn't have." I wondered what was taking the detectives so long. "Will you please check the house so I can go inside? I'm frozen."

"Yes, ma'am," one of the officers stated. "Stay right here."

"Will do." I glanced over to Aaron who was walking back. "Did you reach them?"

"Yes, they're at a restaurant near Lake Minnetonka, a good thirty minutes away, but will head home immediately." He looked at the officer who was studying the window. "I'm Officer Reynolds. I live next door." He pointed to his house. "I'm taking Liv back to my house, if that's okay with you."

"Sure. As long as we know where to find her."

"Let's go." He led me across the yard, through the snow, onto his back steps, then inside.

"Yikes. I'm cold."

"How about a cup of hot chocolate? Got some instant stuff around here somewhere," Aaron sat me by the kitchen table.

"Sounds good. It'll warm me up." I shut my eyes, holding my head between my palms. Suddenly my eyes popped open. "All this mess at the store and the basement commotion, wedding plans. I totally forgot about making sure that Grandpa took care of the cufflinks. Oh my gosh! What if they're stolen?"

"I'm sure they weren't found. Who would look in a birdcage for a pair of cufflinks?" He poured milk in a mug and added a packet of hot chocolate mix, placing it in the microwave. "But, we'll get to the bottom of this, even if we end up raising both Dolley and the President James Madison from the grave."

"Not sure how much else I can stand." I held my breath as Aaron set the hot mug down in front of me. "I hate to say this, but it might come to that. I suppose the detectives will be here soon." I took a sip. "Hot! I wish we knew for certain the motive besides a 'secret'." I blew into the cup. "Scratch that! The motive's greed. 'For the love of money is a root of all kinds of evil.'"

"It's very possible. Feel better?" We heard someone knock. Aaron opened the door, and I listened as Aaron said, "Come in, Detective. We've been waiting."

"Liv, sorry about all of this. You've had it pretty rough going lately." Erlandsen pressed against the countertop. "We've got your statement from the officer, but there's one more request."

"And that is?" I kept my eyes focused on his. "Oh gosh. Something horrible happened."

"Not at all." He shook his head. "We would like you to walk through the house with us. We've checked everything out and nothing looks out of place. If you're ready, that is."

"I'd be more than happy to." I popped up to my feet. "You comin', Aaron?"

"Right behind." He looked at the detective who shook his head. "Guess not. I'll stay in the kitchen."

"Much better."

I grabbed my jacket. Detective Erlandsen opened the door and followed me outside. Aaron trailed behind. The three of us headed across to the back door of Grandma and Grandpa's house just as an officer stepped out. "Detective Mergens is waiting inside."

"Thank you." Erlandsen stepped up the stairs, held open the door as I stepped inside, with Aaron behind me.

"My grandparents will be home shortly," I told him as we walked into the kitchen.

Detective Mergens met me in the living room, where he stood with his arms crossed over his chest. "You've certainly given us plenty to do, Miss Anderson."

"I hate to see people out of work." I knew that he was chiding me.

"I want you to look for anything that seems amiss."

"Anything different, right?"

"Just take your time and study everything," he repeated.

"Where should we begin?" I crossed and uncrossed my arms. "The dining room?"

"Nope. The basement." Detective Mergens looked at me. "Right where it began."

The two detectives followed me over to the basement stairs. The light had burned out, so we descended the dark staircase until we reached the basement, where I flipped on the light switch. A warm glow cast over the cement floor. Over to the left was the laundry area, where shattered glass sparkled against the light beam. The shelves above the laundry tubs held old canning jars. Grandma filled one with detergent for her wash loads rather than pour from the larger container.

"They came in through here, as you know." Mergens walked over to the area near the window. He flicked on another light and focused on an old chair. "Then stepped from the washing machine or dryer down to this chair. A shoe print has been photographed, it's wide and long, like a man's."

"So it was a 'he' that broke in?" I asked, confused. "I thought it may have been a 'she'."

"We've got reason to believe that there were two." Mergens held up two fingers. "A male and a female. A team." He stared at me. "Any thoughts on that?"

"Of course. Wanda and Stone."

"Anything look different down here besides the broken window?" Mergens motioned toward it. "What about by the wine cellar?" We strode over toward it. "You need a password to get inside, I see."

"Yes. Grandpa worried that my friends and I would raid it when I was younger," I chuckled. "Now, I raid it anyway." I entered the code that opened the door. "Looks just fine from here." They peeked inside the door.

"All right. Now for the upstairs."

I locked the wine cellar door and shut off the basement light before walking upstairs. I shut the basement door and followed the detectives into the dining room. We went from room to room in this manner. Every so often, they asked about certain pieces of furniture or wall displays.

"This sampler is a little off-kilter, and shouldn't be." I reached out to straighten it, but Mergens pulled my hand away.

"Those old things are put on frames that aren't properly squared."

I watched him make a notation in his notepad, and then we circled the rest of the living room. I took my time in the small TV room, looking at worn out coffee table magazines, pictures on the walls, and slippers tossed on the floor. A small bookshelf was against the back wall. I studied the few knick-knacks on the shelves, and noticed a small, china flowerpot that didn't look familiar. It was no taller than my hand, with small flowers painted on the perimeter. I pointed to it and Mergens made another notation.

As we were entering the office, I heard Grandpa's voice. Erlandsen left, presumably to prevent them from entering the rest of the house. A fluffy teddy bear sat on the top shelf of the bookcase. It looked cute, but I knew for certain that I'd never seen it before so I pointed to it. Another notation. I nodded at an old cardboard box sitting on the side of the desk.

"Upstairs." Erlandsen motioned for us to leave the room.

As we walked into the living room, my grandparents were entering, and we nodded. Grandma blew me a kiss, which made me smile. I must've looked serious, because that's what she used to do when I had to recite something in school. It helped me forget to be nervous.

Upstairs, we poked inside the two bedrooms and bathroom, but I didn't see anything out of the ordinary. I even opened the linen closet, and the towels appeared undisturbed. Then I glanced upward and stared at the hatch door.

Two prongs were out of position.

After Mergens had made a notation, we went downstairs.

Erlandsen's eyes skimmed over us, and before you knew it, we had gathered in a circle outside on the back deck.

"It appears that your house has been bugged. The items Miss Anderson pointed out lean to that conclusion. We won't know for certain until we look closer." Detective Mergens looked at each of us in turn.

"This is totally mystifying," Grandma said, frowning. "Completely."

"We've picked up letters from an attorney today which my wife has inherited. The cufflinks, I truly didn't believe would put our Olivia's life in jeopardy since the burglary happened some fifty years ago. Also that guy's dead. I'm sorry. They're still in the birdcage in the attic, I believe, or hope," Grandpa said.

"Mr. Ott," Erlandsen said, looking down at his notes. "You'd better put them in the bank first thing in the morning and leave them there until this case gets solved."

"I will."

"There's no known motive, is there?" I stared at Mergens. "No one can figure it out." When they both shook their heads and crossed their arms, I figured it was my turn to take a shot at this.

"I think it dates back to Dolley and James Madison." I closed my mouth, to wait for someone to say something, but neither detective responded. "Jackie Newell asked me if I knew about the family secret. I didn't know what she was talking about, and at that time also did not know that she was a distant relative. She'd grabbed the dolls too, remember?" I saw they were becoming impatient by the way they looked away from me and pretended as if they were listening, when I knew they weren't. "Grandma's sampler is almost identical to the one that's hanging on Alexander Hamilton's wall in New York City."

"Liv, you're digging way too deep here." Erlandsen sighed. "Nothing adds up to a present day murder."

"For goodness sake. Listen to my granddaughter. You don't have any better ideas, do ya, sonny?" Grandma planted her hands on her hips.

"Grandma." I took a deep breath. "A set of rubies and a brooch were stolen from Montpelier. Did you know that?" I pointed my finger at them.

"Liv." Mergens pulled out his notepad. "Okay. I'll play along with you." I watched him scribble a few words.

"A set of cufflinks, which used to belong to President Madison, were bequeathed by Dolley to a Mr. Elijah Putnam."

"He's also a distant relative of mine." Grandpa raised his chin. "I have the cufflinks, remember?"

"Right," Mergens said. "They're still in a birdcage up in the attic."

"This is all just fine and dandy, but how does it relate to a present day murder?" Erlandsen asked.

"That's what we don't know." I massaged my chin. "And, I'm going to find out."

# Chapter Sixteen

"You want us to climb up into the attic before you leave, just to make sure the cufflinks are there?" Aaron had joined us. "It's convoluted, but there are so many coincidences."

"If the cufflinks are gone, then we'll know it's a burglary." Erlandsen stared up at the hatch cover.

"I'll go get the stool, but let me climb up there," I said.

"Let me." Aaron gave me a solemn look. "I don't want anything to happen to you."

"What could possibly happen? There are two detectives plus you, along with my grandparents standing watch." It was true. At that moment, they poked out from the bathroom door where they'd been eavesdropping. The hallway was too small for us all. It took a minute for me to fetch the stool and set it under the hatch. I moved over so Erlandsen could climb up to open the hatch. He'd already removed a pair of plastic gloves from his pocket and slipped them on as he stepped up on the stool.

"Mr. Ott, August, why didn't you ever have stairs put in? It'd be a lot easier," Erlandsen grumbled, pulling the folding stairs down. "I'm curious."

"It's never been a problem." I stood beside Grandpa who shook his head.

"We have really old and valuable papers up there. Love letters from when I was in the Marines plus my bride's wedding gown," Grandpa said.

I glanced over at Grandma, knowing they were the love of each other's life. I trusted Aaron and I would be the same. So much in love for such a long time. It made my heart go pitter-pat. I turned my attention to the trapdoor, wondering what else was hidden up there.

"Liv?" Mergens voice interrupted my thoughts. "The ladder's set. Go get 'em and bring 'em down, if you will?"

"Of course." I climbed the ladder, popped my head into the attic; hauling myself inside. Once standing, I reached for the light string and yanked it. A wave of light brightened the room.

"How's it look?" Mergens' concerned voice below me spoke volumes.

"Fine, as far as I can tell." Gazing around the room I checked the dusty floor for footprints. It didn't seem as if anyone had padded over my earlier footsteps. My shaky fingers cautiously opened the antique birdcage drawer. Closing my eyes, it felt as if my heart stopped beating. I forced myself to look, but there they were, just as before. I let out a long breath of relief before calling, "They're here!"

I carefully placed them in my pants pocket. At the same moment, Aaron's head poked up through the opening. I said, "Let's take that box over there down. I think it's full of letters. I'll hand it to you."

"Anything else that might fit your plot?" Erlandsen asked.

"Listen, mister! Pay attention to my granddaughter!" Grandpa said.

Aaron and I quietly chuckled as I handed him the box. When he'd started down the steps, I found the other box that had caught my interest earlier, and had it ready to hand over to him.

"Where are the detectives?" I whispered to Aaron once his nose poked into the opening.

"I told them to go to my house, but they're still here," he nodded downward, mouthing.

I didn't respond except for handing him the other box. After climbing down, I was ready to tighten the latches to the hatch when Mergens said, "Don't. We'll do that." When I went to pick up the stool, he said, "Leave it."

"Here are the cufflinks." I held them out, and each detective took one to look at.

"They look like the flag but with this imprint around it," Mergens said.

"I can see that they're valuable," Erlandsen said.

"Bank in the morning," Mergens said, placing his in my palm.

"They're too dangerous to keep," Erlandsen said, setting his beside the other one. "I assume, Aaron, that you've invited your future family over for coffee?" Erlandsen asked.

"As a matter of fact, I have. That's where we're going now."

"I'm picking up cousin Nellie's box, which I haven't seen yet. Hold on a sec." I quickly went for it, and met Aaron by the backdoor.

Aaron and I walked over to his house only to find my grandparents curled up on the couch. I sat down beside Grandma, while Aaron went to get a spare chair. We set the boxes on the coffee table.

"One for each?" Grandpa held up a wine bottle and we all nodded except Aaron.

"I work later."

"Thought so." He proceeded to pour. Grandma snuggled closer.

"I feel bad that this had to happen." I took my offered glass and sipped. I removed the cufflinks from my pocket. "I wonder where this will lead us?"

"We know what's on the gadroon, the imprint, which makes me wonder if that isn't what they're after?" Aaron asked.

"Polly. Polly on both." I pulled the cufflinks out of my pocket to hold up for them to get a better look. "I don't see anything different. Thirteen ruby stars."

"Thirteen strawberries." Grandma smiled.

"Thirteen colonies. The making of our country." I gave the cufflinks to Grandpa. "They'll go back inside the desk when we get home and you're placing them in the bank tomorrow morning." I stared at both grandparents. "I'm keeping them right in my pocket, and leaving them there for now."

"The gadroon is what they're after," Grandma said.

"Let's take another angle." My insides were warm and I felt cozy because now we all believed the crime revolved around Dolley Madison. "I believe it's time to read these letters."

"You're not going to read our love letters!" Grandpa declared, and his eyes became as big as plates. "You wouldn't dare. Marie!" He stared at Grandma. "Do something."

"Settle down, you two." Aaron grinned. "We found an older box that was hidden further in the back, behind others. Don't worry. We'd never read your letters, at least not until you're both gone. Then we'll print them in the newspaper."

"We'll give them to Ronnie." I glanced out the window, noticed the detectives walking over to the house. I grimaced.

"Aaron, they're here."

"I'll let them in." He got up and went to the door. "Have a seat."

They both remained standing.

"Chilly out. Brrr!" Detective Erlandsen said. "I suggest you remain here until we're done next door, unless you need to do something, of course." He glanced at the decorated tree from the living room. "Let's hope that this gets wrapped up before the holidays."

*I figured him as the nicest of the two detectives, also the most under-standing.*

"We hope so too," Grandma stated.

"Don't worry, we get the drill." I wondered if they would bring in those two suspects for more questioning. I hoped they would. "Will you question Stone and Wanda again?"

"If we can locate them."

"Max found them at a sleaze motel by the University. Try looking up rented vehicles."

"We're on it, Liv. Stay out of it."

"What's in the box?" Detective Erlandsen nodded to the inherited, cousin Nellie's box.

"We don't know yet." I began removing the lid. "I think they're over a hundred years old. Not sure."

"We need clean hands, my dear." Grandma gave me a stern look. "They shouldn't be exposed to the air."

"You're right. We should wear gloves." I knew where to find a couple pairs too. Grandma had white gloves in the trunk at the foot of her bed.

"On the off-chance that there might be something to all of this," Erlandsen cleared his throat and loosened his tie, "I contacted the Montpelier (duPont) museum security officer to inquire about the break-in that Liv mentioned, and also asked what's missing. I found out Jackie Newell was also there the day it happened."

"They can prove that?" Aaron asked. "We've searched the Internet. We already knew she was in the area."

"I figured she was the burglar."

"Hmm." Erlandsen massaged his chin. "What about her entourage? I think I'll give 'em another call in the morning."

"Good idea, Detective."

"We'll stay in touch."

We looked at each other as if frozen when the detective left the room.

"I hope it won't be much longer until we can go home." I glanced at the time on my phone. It was already eight o'clock.

"I really need to sleep, guys. Liv?" He leaned over and kissed me. "Good night. I'll text later." To the three of us, he said, "Just lock up when you leave."

"We will. Good night, honey." I watched him go up his stairs. "I can't believe that I'm sitting here like this."

"Neither can we."

Minutes slowly passed, as I stared at the boxes.

"I'm calling a detective." I placed the call, and asked, "May I sneak in for a pair of gloves and leave right away?"

"Back door. No talking."

"Got it." I took a breath and said, "You guys stay here. I'm going over to get the gloves, and to see what's happening. I'll return in a jiffy." I handed the remote to Grandma, who flicked on the TV as I slipped into my jacket.

I trudged across the yard, went in the back door, and straight to the living room, where I found the two forensic men waving electronic devices over picture frames and lamps. When they saw me they both shook their heads.

When Mergens removed the sampler from the wall and turned it over, my eyes opened wide as he removed a device. He held it to the light before dropping it into a plastic bag, and labeling it. Almost immediately, he held up his finger as if to say 'hold on', and then both detectives went outside. I figured they brought all the evidence out to the squad car.

I hurried upstairs to fetch the gloves and came back down. Erlandsen followed me to the kitchen and outside on the steps. After closing the door, he said, "You're safe now."

"Is it full of bugs?"

"Not anymore. I'll give the house another run-through, but I think we've found all the devices." Detective Erlandsen held up a finger as he began listing where all the devices were located. "The office phone had one. There was a teddy bear on a shelf, kind of hidden behind some books, which is why some of you may not have suspected it, or flat didn't see it. Also, the device behind the wall sampler." He held up three fingers. "Can ya think of anyone who would do this?"

"Lots, but it all comes back to Jackie Newell's entourage." I swallowed hard. "I'll be at Aaron's next door with my grandparents. Just walk in when you're finished."

"Got it. It won't take long," Erlandsen said. "We'll make another sweep, then we'll be done."

After reentering the house, I sat back down.

"Let's wait to look at the letters. I think we'll be able to go home soon."

Worry had beset us, so we were all happy to go back home when Erlandsen called ten minutes later and gave us the green light. Grandpa reached for the jackets, Grandma grabbed one of the boxes while I picked up the other. We headed straight for the office and placed the boxes on the floor near the desk.

For the first few minutes, I thought about the evening and how it was shattered. "I feel violated." I stared at Grandma. "Don't you?"

"I think we all do." Grandpa looked out the window. "The police are finally starting to consider the Madison theory, at least." He raised his eyes to look at me. "What do you think, Livvie, honey?"

"I believe this reaches far back into history." I reached for a sheet of paper and wrote: thirteen colonies. "I believe that all those thirteens are symbolic of the colonies. If that's true, then we are talking about Dolley."

"I agree with Olivia." Grandma always called me Olivia when she had too much to drink or was overly tired. "Dolley took pleasure in everything. As a Quaker, she knew how to embroider beautifully. You should Google the history of embroidery. That might answer a few questions."

"I already planned to."

"Morning comes too early." Grandpa yawned. "It's close to eleven. Past my bedtime."

"Mine too." Grandma stood and reached for Grandpa's hand.

"Good night, you two." I got up to kiss them good night. I hustled downstairs to turn on the DVD to watch another Mitch Miller Sing-A-Long Show. I sat cousin Nellie's box in front of the television. I carefully lifted the cover and peered in. It was filled with old, yellowed envelopes. I slipped on the gloves, picked up an envelope, and pulled the letter from it. It read:

> *My Dearest Sister, 1816*
>> *I missed you something fierce when I traveled to New York City. The City has vastly changed since last visited. Mrs. Hamilton adored my gift, and hung it on her wall for all to see. She is a lovely woman.*

*How are you? You must come and visit Mr. Madison and myself, of course! We will soon leave Washington City for Montpelier. I do so look forward to the change as the President's City becomes so stifling in the summer months.*
*Praise God!*
*Dolley Madison*

I almost fell off the chair from shock. Neatly, I folded the letter in the same exact fold and slid it back into the envelope. I filed it back with the other letters. As I searched through the stack of letters, I found several addressed envelopes dated from 1812–1817. I assumed they were written by Dolley. I removed the top letters and, one by one, opened them for a read.

*Dearest Sister, 1815*
*I believe that you offer a greater suggestion than what I could ever come up with on my own. What a brilliant idea! Brilliant! It'll add symbolism. What a glorious conception. Everyone will know what thirteen references. The hardest part of the whole ide, will be where to hide it.*
*Polly will be the death of me yet. He just flew outside and the slave is running after him. Good grief! It's a sight to behold! He's running with a net!*
*Your loving sister,*
*Dolley M*

I was unsure what to do. I was afraid to leave the letters sit in the box like they had for all these years. I carefully placed the letters inside a plastic bag and between the pages of a paperback book and hid it.

I glanced over to the TV only to see the bouncing ball skip across the words to *Yellow Rose of Texas*. I shut off the television and went up to bed.

As I crawled under the covers, I replayed the memory of my favorite basketball game. No one knocked the ball out from under me.

# Chapter Seventeen

I opened the store earlier than usual the following morning.

"Good morning, ladies!" I called. I circled the houses, straightened dolls, and furnishings. "You girls look happy. It's nice to be in your home again, isn't it?"

The next thing I did was start the computer humming. I logged into the Montpelier site and composed an e-mail to a historian at Montpelier, Mr. Strowbridge.

> *Dear Mr. Strowbridge,*
>
> *I am distantly related to Dolley Madison via her sister, Anna. In my possession, I have a sampler that we tend to believe was embroidered by Dolley. Do you have a sampler from her collection that has a flag, rose, or marigolds in opposite corners? Could you tell me, also, if the borders have strawberries? If you do have a sampler similar to this design, would you please send a photo of it to me? I'm quite curious.*
>
> *Also, I believe that we have the cufflinks that are in question. My grandfather, August Ott, was distantly related to Mr. Elijah Putnam.*
>
> *Sincerely,*
>
> *Olivia Anderson*

After rereading the letter, I pressed the send button and watched it disappear into cyberspace. At the same moment, Max entered.

"Did you hear about last night? Someone broke into the house through the basement window."

"What next?" He leaned into the counter and flashed those beautiful baby blue eyes at me. "Is anything missing? You didn't get hurt, did you?"

"Not at all, but thanks for asking." I smiled up at him. "We spent the whole evening at Aaron's as the police searched the house. It was long and drawn out. They even checked for listening devices."

"Find any?"

"Yep!" I continued, "The detectives found a listening device behind the sampler, the office phone was bugged, along with a hidden video camera on an office shelf." I waited a moment, and said, "They did find a picture that may help the investigation. Don't know for sure. It's kind of early to know."

"At least some good may come of it." Max scratched his chin. "The person who broke in through the basement window must've just done it. You were lucky to not have spooked him, or you could've been the next victim."

"The attic latches were twisted, but there was no sign of anyone entering it. Thank God." I took a deep breath.

"How long have they been in the family?"

"I think for over 150 years. I want Aaron to wear them at our wedding."

"Now that would be special."

"Then they'll go to the museum, where they belong."

"Good." He started moving away. "By the way, I've got a line on some new doll heads that might be cheaper. I'll keep you posted."

"All right." I logged out of the Internet and checked for e-mail before getting up.

Max continued out the back door.

As I stared at the dollhouses in the backroom my thoughts circled to the rose garden design and how it'd affect the layout on the tables. I didn't want the garden to upstage the houses. I needed plenty of plants with various color, so I pulled the boxes of miniature roses as well as the juniper bushes off the shelf. The time sped past quickly. Aaron had texted me during the night, stating that he'd take me to lunch. Later, Grandma and I had to meet with the caterers. Tomorrow, we would formally send the invitations, even though most guests had already been invited verbally. Hazel, Ronnie's mom, lined up her granddaughter Jessica for the wedding music, and I was planning to meet with her in the morning.

My phone rang and I glanced at the number. "Yes, Grandma?" She was calling to remind me of the meeting with the caterer. We disconnected and I continued working.

Aaron came in the back door just as I was putting the boxes back on the shelves. "Hey, you." He came over and kissed me. "How's your morning going?"

"No problems. I told Max about last night and he didn't have anything to offer." I shrugged my coat on and grabbed my bag. "No one's come in today. No one knows we're open anymore after all the investigations and store closing. I'll have to really hit the ads when we return from our honeymoon. We'll only be gone for an extended weekend, right?"

"We'll ask Marie to come in for you but, Max will be able to fill in also. He does all right. They can always call with questions." Aaron took my arm and we walked together into the brisk air. "Let's walk down the block to get a burger. I'm hungry for one."

"I sure hope we don't get a winter snowstorm the day of our wedding." Arm in arm we walked to the end of the block and entered the restaurant. "Let's pray for a beautiful wedding day." I looked up toward him and we kissed.

Glancing around at the customers, I stopped to also study the wall pictures, which made me think about the room below our feet. *How many people knew about it?*

The waitress came right away and we ordered. As we sat looking out, we watched people jogging and walking over the Stone Arch Bridge. Our conversation turned to the past evening.

"My plan was to research vintage embroidery and search for samples of Dolley's handwriting, but Max walked in. As soon as I see my way clear, I'm going to the Minnesota Historical Center and research Dolley Madison's handwriting." I smiled as two lovers strolled past. "I did, however, send an email to Montpelier about the sampler. I asked for a photo if they had a similar one, and also told them about the cufflinks."

"Once we learn if there is a similar sampler, we'll know we're heading in the right direction." Aaron shook his head and grinned. "Who'd have thought, after all this time, the Father of the Constitution would be knocking on our door?"

The waitress brought our drinks, and before long our burger baskets arrived. We began to eat straightaway.

"I feel as if Grandma and Grandpa will end up being the key to it all." I chewed on a bite of hamburger, and then remembered the letters in my bag. "I read a couple of the letters last night that were in that box Grandma inherited, cousin Nellie's. I had wanted to wait for you to be there, but curiosity got the best of me. Do you want to see them later?"

"Sure, but go on." He studied me as he ate. "I'm listening."

"The letters were from Dolley. I haven't told anyone about these, not even them." I meant my grandparents. "I'm glad that these are unknown as well as unlike the cufflinks."

"Yes, it's one less thing that the killer knows about."

"This is true. Never considered that." I turned my thoughts back to Grandma and how she'd speak about her parents and grandparents. "I haven't read from the other boxed package of letters which we brought down to view."

"There must be a lot, they wrote letters constantly."

"The slaves delivered letters when there wasn't nearby postal service. People had to work at staying in touch."

"Exactly." Aaron bit into his burger. "Chores to do constantly, plus their school work was much tougher than nowadays. If you didn't get one-hundred percent, the teacher might smack you a good one with a ruler."

"How awful. Thank heavens it's a gentler world today." We finished our meal and headed back to the store, stopping by his car. "I'll call when I get home. It shouldn't take long at the caterers. I'm also picking up cookies and cider for the First Lady December birthday celebration on Friday."

We kissed before I went back inside. I got busy arranging the rose garden setting in front of the two 1814 houses. The phone rang a few times and one prospective customer entered. When I finally glanced up at the clock, it was time for me to meet Grandma.

I locked the front door, grabbed my stuff, and was headed out the backdoor when my cell phone rang. It was Dorrie. She apologized for her outburst and asked if she could come to work tomorrow. I said, "Sure, why not?" before disconnecting. I felt sorry for her. Being questioned by the police was an awful experience and she'd gone through it twice.

*Besides, aren't you supposed to keep your enemies closer than friends? What if she does know something about the murder and isn't telling? Maybe she is the murderer?* Chills swept through me as I started my car.

The drive to the caterers brought me not too far from home. We always tried to keep our business local, and the caterer was a neighbor who recently started in the catering business. The location was right across the street from the Riverview Theater. The short strip mall hosted a variety of businesses: Ingrid's Bakery, Swen and Lina's Café and Jeanette's Hairnet. A small coffee shop was right around the corner. I needed to pick up my order of cookies and planned to bring a cup of coffee with me to my meeting with Ingrid. I found myself parking next to Grandma's car.

I got a text message from Debbie while I waited for my coffee. My dress was ready and she wanted to know when we would come and pick it up. I texted Maggie, and we decided to go there as soon as I finished with the caterer.

"Hi, Ingrid. I'll take the cookies if you have them ready." I walked into the bakery with my full coffee cup in hand. Grandma gave me a smile. "What are you two brewing up?" I grinned as I sipped. It felt so good to think about my wedding instead of all the nasty things that had happened recently. "I vote for prime rib and shrimp scampi. I don't want anything too stressful or hard to eat. Everything should be simple."

"We figured as much, honey. The cookies are right here." Ingrid smiled at me and touched the large box on the counter. "Thirty bucks even."

"Here." I reached inside my bag and handed her the cash. "Thanks."

"You're welcome. I'm so glad that you two are finally tying the knot. You've loved each other forever." She came out from behind the glass case, kissed my cheek, and hugged me. "Thanks for choosing me to cater too."

"Wouldn't have it any other way, dear." Grandma stared at the featured wedding cakes inside the case. "They look yummy." She licked her lips.

"Nowadays, the girls prefer either a variety of cheesecakes or cupcakes. What would you like, honey?" Ingrid looked at me. "We can do both."

"Raspberry cheesecake and chocolate, plus assorted cupcake flavors. We must have strawberry for Aaron, so let's have three cheesecakes. They won't go to waste." I smiled, and thought of tasting each.

"Got that down." Ingrid took out her order form booklet and jotted down the deserts. "For the main meal, prime rib and shrimp scampi. Right?" I nodded. "Potatoes?"

"Rice, baked potatoes and all the garnishes. I want to use real china and cloth napkins too. I'm particular about that. It needs to be elegant."

"We'll use our chinaware, dear." Grandma thought a moment. "Let's have the caterers wear those tall white hats and aprons. That'll make it special."

"Of course." Ingrid's eyes lit up like fireworks. "You've been such wonderful neighbors. Now you're using my service for catering, I'd do anything for you."

"You're sweet." My phone buzzed and I listened to the voice mail. "I forgot. I have to go to pick up my dress. Maggie's coming with. I've got to run." I kissed them both, grabbed the cookies, and hurried toward the door.

"What about the veggies and salads?" Ingrid called out to me.

"Grandma can take care of that. I like corn and Aaron likes green beans. Fresh lettuce and coleslaw would be just fine." I knew Grandma had her own ideas, and sooner or later, Ingrid would be asking about the murder and break-in. I was surprised that she hadn't yet, since we'd known each other forever. "I'll call."

After walking out, I gave Aaron a quick call, telling him what I was doing. He and Tim would meet Maggie and me for dinner at a newly opened neighborhood restaurant, Arthur's on Lake. It was located right off Bloomington Avenue and Lake Street.

Maggie lived close by, so it didn't take me long to pick her up. I parked out front and beeped my horn. She came out in a matter of a few minutes.

"I'm so excited," Maggie said, jumping into the car. "Your dress, and mine. This is going to be such a beautiful wedding. I like that it's small."

"It'll be intimate," I said.

"I heard that your best man split with his girlfriend," Maggie said, her face flushed when I nodded.

"Yep."

"I thought so."

"Peggy's dead in the water. I think it's a good thing. We're meeting the guys for dinner at Arthur's. We need to discuss the wedding," I said.

"Good idea."

The rush hour traffic was thick, making it hard to change lanes and exit where we needed to. Eventually, I exited onto Lyndale and drove through the neighboring side streets to get to Debbie's shop.

Debbie greeted us at the door and brought us to the sewing room in the back where our dresses hung. My mouth dropped open as I pictured my mother wearing the dress, and my dad's heart filling with love when he saw her coming down the aisle. I thought of Aaron and how he'd do the same when he saw me in that dress.

"Let's start with the bride," Debbie stated. "It's turned out beautiful, hasn't it?"

"Yes." I could barely speak as I went into the dressing room and removed my clothes, then let Debbie help me draw the dress over my arms and down my torso, zipping it up the back. It fit slightly snug, so I told myself no more chocolate until after the ceremony. Guess I should get out and do some more running.

"This is perfect." I held my breath as Debbie attached the lace-flowered train, which had pearl beads sewn into the design. As I stared at myself in the mirror, I wondered if my mother was watching? Debbie helped me undress, then assisted Maggie.

As I sat waiting for Maggie to step out of the cubicle, I thought about the upcoming evening. I usually didn't believe in blind dates, but this dinner with Tim and Maggie began to sound wonderful. Their names, Maggie and Tim, sounded good together. I wondered if Aaron had this in mind when he suggested that we have dinner? Probably not, I decided, because men didn't think of blind dates or how names sounded together. I looked up as Maggie stepped out of the dressing room.

"That color is perfect on you," I gushed. My eyes opened wide as she turned sideways. "Oh yes, Tim will take notice. I promise."

"The bust is a little tight," Maggie said. "Don't know what to do about that."

"Give some to me," I giggled.

"Hold on a minute. I'll fix it." Debbie held pins in one hand, with a couple poking out from between her lips.

When the nips and tucks were orchestrated and the dresses bagged, I paid the bill. We arranged the dresses carefully in the back of the car and jumped inside. I sent Aaron another message stating that we were on our way to meet them.

The traffic was even worse than before and entering the interstate wasn't easy, nor was exiting onto Bloomington Avenue. An abundance of stoplights and turning cars brought the flow of traffic to almost a standstill. Finally we made it, and I parked across the street from the restaurant, right behind Tim's Chevy. We climbed out, walked up the street, and entered Arthur's.

Tim and Aaron stood to the side in the entry, waiting for us.

"You're glowing," Aaron whispered in my ear, when he kissed me.

"I know. I can feel it." All I could think about was being alone with him.

The hostess came over with the menus, and asked, "Ready?"

"You betcha," Tim responded.

We wound through cloth-covered, candlelit tables until eventually the hostess seated us at a corner table near a window. The lights from Lake Street added romance to the air, sparkling like diamonds.

"I wish there was a veranda at Grandma and Grandpa's." I sighed, thinking of my wedding.

"That would be nice." Maggie and Tim stared at each other, and I realized for certain that they'd make a great couple.

The men ordered the wine before we began talking about the wedding. The evening slipped by gracefully and quickly. Too soon we were paying our bill and heading out to the cars. Maggie climbed in with Tim, and Aaron drove my car.

"I forgot to check my messages. Mind if I do?" I placed my head on Aaron's shoulder.

"Go ahead." He waited to drive away until after Tim drove out.

I retrieved my cell phone from my bag, pressed the voice message button and opened it. The voice said:

*Miss Anderson,*

> *We need to speak privately and on a secure phone. It's very important. Have your attorney contact me at this number. We'll set up a date when we can meet and I can inspect the package. From now on, they'll be referred to as 'package'.*
>
> *Dolley embroidered many samplers in her day. They were like a family history. If I'm correct, then I believe that we have a similar one and it is in storage. I will send an image from a printed copy, which is also sold in the gift shop.*
>
> *I look forward to hearing from your attorney.*

*Don Strowbridge.*

My heart pounded. "Did you hear that?" I looked at Aaron. "Open up the picture."

I fumbled with the buttons as I opened the image.

It was identical to Grandma's sampler, except the fourth square motif was a tombstone.

# Chapter Eighteen

"A tombstone? I don't believe it," I gasped. "I'm going to make drawings of each of them. It'll make more sense."

"What about the other three corners?" Aaron asked.

"Marigolds." I thought a moment. "Hamilton's had the rose in the upper left. Grandma's in the upper right has the flag. This one, the bottom right has the tombstone."

"Go figure." I yawned. "Then we have the cufflinks. How do they fit into the picture? The gadroon? What about that imprint? Polly? Why a bird's name?"

"Your guess is as good as mine." He started the car. "August won't be happy to relinquish them." Aaron gave me a concerned look as we waited for a light to turn green. "But the cufflinks should be donated, if they're found to be authentic." He started driving. "I wonder if the Putnam family has knowledge of them?"

"Grandpa is the Putnam family. They were passed down to him." I drew in a deep breath.

"After all these years, their secret is out. The Putnam letter, plus the true ownership of the cufflinks." Aaron kept his eyes on the road. "We'll have to have our attorney, Mr. Nye, do the legal paperwork for turning it over to the museum. They really do belong to your grandpa, since he's the rightful heir."

"Let's wait until tomorrow." I coyly looked at him.

"Sounds good to me."

The following morning, I met my grandparents in the kitchen as they were having breakfast.

"Morning." I gave them each a kiss on the cheek. "We had a great time. The dresses are hung in my closet." I dropped a slice of bread into the toaster and began pouring a glass of orange juice.

"How'd they fit?" Grandma asked.

"Like a glove. Maggie's beautiful."

"How was dinner?" Grandma asked.

"We had a great time. I think Maggie and Tim hit it off." My thoughts went to how I noticed their nonchalant touching, plus all those glances over the glasses at each other. "Maggie smiled a lot."

"What about Tim?" Grandma asked.

"He seemed just as happy."

"I can see you have something else on your mind, Olivia." Grandpa stood beside Grandma. "I'd like to hear what it is."

"Don Strowbridge from Montpelier sent a request for us to contact our attorney about the cufflinks. He wants to see them and also has a few questions." My eyes strayed from one to the other. Grandma looked satisfied. "Also, the two letters I read the night before last were signed in Dolley's name. How could your cousin not tell you about them, or your mother?" I leaned into the counter. "Is there anything else about either lineage that you're not telling me? Now's the time."

"Should we say something or not, August?" Grandma glanced up at him.

"What do you mean? Should we or shouldn't we? There's no question here!" I banged my fist on the counter.

"Well, all right. There is a letter. The original from Dolley where she asked him to—"

"I thought it was from the Putnams, thanking her for the gift." I held my hand up like a stop sign. "You mean to tell me that you've been hanging on to this letter the whole time and never told me about it? Did my mother know about it too?"

169

"We haven't told anyone. She didn't know. It's been our secret because of the value of it, and it's proved ownership." Grandma hung her head. "Forgive me, Olivia. We're really sorry."

"Why am I always the last person to find out?" I shook my head. "So—where is this letter of ownership from Dolley?" I stared at Grandpa and then Grandma. "Where?"

"Calm down, for heaven's sake, Olivia." Grandpa looked away for a moment. "It's sealed in an envelope in the safety deposit box with the cufflinks. No one else knows about it. Or should I say no one did except Grandma—now you."

"Your mother was a snoop. That's why the letter went into the bank. The cufflinks should've been too. We know that now." Grandma reached for Grandpa's hand. "It will be hard to give the cufflinks up, but they should be donated to the Montpelier museum. It's the rightful place, honey." She squeezed Grandpa's hand. "Right?"

"Aaron wanted to wear them for the wedding." Grandpa looked me square in the eye. "What's your take on that?"

"I believe that he should. I'd like him to. Maybe we could have the meeting with Don Strowbridge after the wedding?"

"We'll call Mr. Nye right away, and he'll take it from there."

"Sounds good." I bit into my cold toast. "We'll leave it all in the bank."

I finished my breakfast, grabbed my bag, and headed out the door.

Once parked out back, I entered the store and headed straight to Dolley. "Would you please tell me what one earth you were thinking when you embroidered the samplers? Why are the corners different? Why bouncing strawberries, and the number thirteen? I'm totally puzzled." I held the doll and stared into the tiny eyes. "I wish that you could speak and tell me your secrets." I set the doll into position as the door opened, and Dorrie entered.

She hung the pictures and set the Penny dolls back on the shelves. I busied myself by arranging the dollhouse displays and reordering the inventory that needed replacing. Grandpa found someone to come in and make a bid for securely locking the trapdoor. Hopefully it would be completed by the end of next week.

It was great having Dorrie back to work. She looked after customers, which left me time to take care of other matters.

By the end of the week, it had been settled about the cufflinks. Since Grandpa's cufflinks initially belonged to Dolley, Aaron would wear them for the wedding. An official from Montpelier and one of their security guards would also attend the ceremony. Afterwards, the Montpelier representatives would take the cufflinks to the estate. Mr. Nye recommended that we pay for a police officer to also attend. I knew these cufflinks were valuable, but all of these security precautions made me nervous. Very nervous. I started biting my nails and chewing on my hair. That nervous.

The next few days flew past and my thoughts were completely on my wedding. Even as I set out the tiny rosebushes in the dollhouse gardens and lined them with appropriate trees, I thought about my wedding. The horses and carriages added a nice touch to the scenery.

Finally Friday rolled around with the grand birthday celebration for the First Ladies born in December, beginning with Lady Bird Johnson. Several new customers happened in at the same time. Dorrie managed with the two interested in the recent Bush First Ladies.

"How did Barbara Bush break her wrist?" one of the women asked.

"Sliding with her grandchildren."

"Was Laura Bush really a librarian?"

"Of course? Both were interested in literacy."

An older woman was concerned about Edith Wilson, the Suffragist movement, and how the White House managed with the President so ill during the war. First Lady Wilson took care of correspondence, and kept the President abreast of all things, I told her.

The day sped by quickly and easily. I was exhausted at the close of the day, but tonight was my bachelorette party.

"See you later," I said to Dorrie. "The burgers are on me tonight. You've been a huge help today. I sincerely thank you."

"Glad to help. See you later."

I watched Dorrie go out the back door as I closed up the store for the night. The bachelorette party was set to start in an hour. We three girls—Maggie, Dorrie, and I—decided to wear matching shirts, which read: *Bring It On!* Why on earth we chose that saying was beyond me, but Dorrie wanted them to read: *The BUST sisters.* I drew the line on that one.

I had just enough time to shower and get over to Margie's Bar.

Though I parked in the back alley parking lot, I got out of the car and walked around to the front entrance. Country music blared from the jukebox, and the bar was lined with people enjoying Friday night happy hour. Bottles and glasses cluttered the bar as well as the booths I passed by. Dorrie and Maggie were seated in a back booth; I crawled in beside Maggie.

"Sorry for running late. I feel like I'm going around in circles." I looked up and caught the waitress' eye. She came right over and we ordered a pitcher of beer.

"Are you and Tim getting together later?" I nudged Maggie. "Or aren't you telling?" Maggie's dark hair looked silky, and she'd brought one side back behind her ear. Her brown eyes and thick lashes looked more sensual than normal. I decided that she'd applied extra makeup to get that effect. Her bright red lipstick with silver undertones added to the bedtime mood. I figured Tim didn't stand a chance against this girl. Tonight was the night.

"We thought we'd play it by ear." She gave me a coy look. I knew what she was thinking. His place.

"Brad is picking me up." Dorrie looked the other way before looking back at me. "We're going to cruise the town."

"Cruise around?" I raised a brow. "Brad? As in the chauffeur." I glanced at Maggie. "And, you two are married, but didn't tell us."

"You've always been secretive. Where did you meet him and how do you know him? And who in Sam Hill is he?" Maggie asked. "It's girls' night out. Time to spill the beans. Did you elope? How long did you know him? Who is he, anyway?"

"He made me promise to keep it secret, because of how it might affect Liv." Dorrie glanced at me.

"I'm okay with it. I'm sure his grandparents didn't mean to crash into my parents and kill them, but let's not talk about the accident nor my parents. I want to hear about where you married and why there's no ring on your finger?"

"We married a couple months ago. We went to the JP. The Justice of the Peace. He's a student who chauffeurs for a job. That's about it," Dorrie said.

The waitress brought over the beer, and poured our glasses full before leaving.

"Where are you going on your honeymoon?" Dorrie took a sip and stared at me. "You've never said."

"We're not through asking you questions. Where will you go on your honeymoon?" I wondered if she purposely changed the subject? "What is Brad like? Quiet? Shy? He looks like he was a wrestler in high school."

"He was a wrestler. I suppose his muscles gave him away. He can get quiet and can be stubborn and ornery at times, then sweet. Mostly he's easy to get along with, but money is always a problem. I can't wait for him to graduate, then get a job so we can have kids."

"His degree is in?"

"He hasn't made up his mind. It's either criminal justice or education, but school loans keep stacking up. We're in the hole so deep already. Don't know where the money's going to come from to pay it all back. For both of our loans, we owe almost a hundred thousand." She glanced over to Maggie. "It's her turn now to tell us where she's going on her honeymoon."

"Yeah. Where is Aaron skirting you off to?" Maggie giggled. "No pun intended!"

"He's never said. I've asked, but he won't tell me. It's a secret." My phone chirped, and I took it out and read the message. *R u hav fn.* "He wants to know if we're having fun." I sent back one which read, *Y.* "I told him, 'yes'."

"Ask him about the honeymoon," Dorrie pressed. "I want to know."

"We'll find out soon enough." I glanced toward the bar and the waitress came over. "We'd all three like Juicy Lucy burgers, right?"

"With fries?"

"Of course!" we said in unison.

"And another pitcher?"

"Yep."

"Aaron will be as handsome as can be wearing his tux," Maggie said. "Will he wear the cufflinks?"

"It's up to him," I said. I didn't want anyone to know for sure because of their value. Glancing at the door, a man and a woman who seemed familiar were entering, but I couldn't place them. "You see those two over there?" I asked, and nodded toward them. "The woman is short and wearing glasses, the man is taller. Why are they so familiar looking?"

"I have no idea." Maggie shrugged. "Maybe they're former customers?"

"I think I'd remember." I chewed on the tip of a clump of my red hair. I glanced over at them again, but they'd moved to another section.

"Here comes the food." Dorrie immediately reached into the French fry basket and began munching. "Really good." She squirted ketchup on the side of her basket and onto the burger.

"No one makes a burger like these, anyplace. The middle cheese layer is enough to die for." Maggie took a huge bite. "There goes my diet."

"You have no worries, honey, you're tall and thin. I'm the one who should worry." I bit into my burger and swooned. It was delicious.

As we ate, both Dorrie and Maggie received text messages.

"I think the guys miss us," I stated as I chewed. "They can't live without us."

"Nor us, them."

"Tell me more about the wedding? Are you wearing your mom's dress?" Dorrie asked.

"I've had it fitted." I grinned. "Aaron's wearing something from Dad."

"That's wonderful," Maggie said. "I bet it's the cufflinks."

"We're donating them to Montpelier. I took another large bite of my burger and nodded.

About the time that we were finishing our burgers, the waitress came over with three drinks from the bar. She set them down.

"Who sent them?"

"The guy wants to remain anonymous."

"We're getting ready to leave," I remarked. "Send them back. You can bring our tab." I knew better than to accept drinks from strangers. Dating a cop, you learn about all sorts of date rape drugs.

"If you say so, hon, but I'm sure he won't like it." She shrugged. "Be right back." She walked away.

The clock read eight when we stepped out onto the street-lit sidewalk. The December days were short, and the sun had already set.

"Good night." Dorrie stood beside her car.

"Wish me luck." Maggie opened her car door.

"You won't need it. I think it's already in the bag. Night!" I waved to both, and then went behind the building to the back parking lot. Shadows covered the lot, which was now filled with trucks and cars. A loud crunch of gravel was startling. I wondered if someone was following me. I quickly turned to look. *Were those footsteps I heard?* I kept going, and the crunching became louder. I hurried my steps. My heart pounded, and with trembling fingers, I pulled my keys from my bag.

Fear zipped up and down my spine when I reached for the door and quickly climbed inside, and immediately locking the door. I started the car and hurried home, sending a message to Aaron to meet me there. Headlights followed me home. It was an unrecognizable car. After driving around the block a couple times to veer them from my final destination, I lost them. My grandparents didn't like for me to park in the garage, but I did anyway. As soon as I'd shut off the engine, I let out a very long sigh of relief.

After climbing from the car, I went over to the back garage windows and peeked out. I didn't see headlights or nearby cars so I sneaked out and raced up to the house.

As I stuck the key into the door, I heard footsteps once again—and froze. What seemed like forever, I waited. When I didn't hear anything I finished opening the door and slipped inside. Before I could lock it, the door crashed into me.

"Where are they?" Wanda held me at knife point. "Now! Liv! You took the dolls. You have the cufflinks. Give them to us, now!"

"Yes. What's on that brooch?" Stone moved closer from behind. I felt his breath on my shoulders.

"What are you talking about?" I started backing up, hoping that Grandma hadn't cleaned up the kitchen. *There has to be a frying pan in the sink.* "My fiancé is due any time."

"You don't have a clue, do you?" Wanda swung the knife, and jabbed me on the arm. "The secret." Her voice shrilled. "Tell us."

"I don't know." I kept my eyes steady in hers. Stone reached out, and pulled my hair, snapping my head backward.

"It was you. You assaulted me. The gorilla-man."

"Huh," he chuckled, pulling my head back further.

Wanda let her arm down and glanced around the room, and it gave me a moment to act. I kicked my foot up, connecting with his inner thigh, which loosened his grip so I could get away from him.

"You bitch." He slapped me across the face as Wanda held the knife against my throat.

"I'm not through with you." I thought I heard Aaron on the steps, but wasn't sure. I dared a chance look in the sink, and saw the small fry pan used for an egg. Instantly, I reached for it, swung around and whacked her on the side of the head. The knife flew, hit the floor, and slid across it. Stone lurched for me just as Aaron opened the door and leaped for him, tackling him down to the floor. I stomped my foot on Wanda's hair.

At the same time, sirens blared, and stopped outside.

Two officers entered, easily subduing the two and taking them out in handcuffs. Back-up squad cars came and hauled them away. In just a few minutes, it became question and answer time.

"From the top, ma'am," the officer stated.

"You really need to contact Detectives Erlandsen and Mergens."

"Why's that ma'am?"

"Because they're working a case which involves these two criminals.

"Yes, ma'am."

"If I may interject," Aaron cleared his throat, "I've contacted them. I'm a police officer." He showed his badge. "They're on their way."

"Good."

"We also need your statement, sir." The line of questioning was diverted to Aaron.

"May I contact my grandparents now? They need to know what's happened. They're at some kind of garden club meeting."

"Go ahead."

I went out to the living room and gave Grandma a call. "Grandma?" I drew in a deep breath before continuing, "Wanda and Stone followed me home."

"We're leaving. That's it," Grandma replied.

"The police have them already in custody. Aaron's here with me. The police are questioning him at the moment."

"Sit down and put on *I Love Lucy*. We'll be home soon."

"Okay." We disconnected and I did as told, but couldn't find the Lucy show. I was surfing the channels when Aaron entered.

"The detectives are just pulling up."

"Let them in." I got up. "I'm putting on a pot of coffee."

"Yes, I think it'll be a long night." He held me in his arms. "What a mess."

"Yes," I responded. "Now it's time to catch the killer."

"They just did," Aaron said.

"Not by a long shot."

# Chapter Nineteen

We'd congregated in the kitchen to discuss the matter when we noted the detectives arriving by the backdoor. The squad car was still parked and the attending officer met them as they'd parked and got out of their car.

"They didn't ask the right question."

"What are you talking about?" Aaron asked. "You don't make any sense. They just carted away the killers. Now you're saying that they aren't the killers? Then who are they?"

"They are Jackie Newell's employees, hired to get their hands on the dolls and to locate the cufflinks, but Jackie didn't steal the brooch from the museum."

I opened the door to allow the detectives to enter. "We're having a discussion about the killers. I say that Wanda and Stone aren't, because they didn't ask the right question."

"How do you know that?" Erlandsen asked. He leaned against the kitchen counter. "I don't understand."

"This case has me stymied, I must admit," Mergens grumbled.

"You're not alone on that thought," Aaron said.

"Let's go and sit down in the living room." Grandma ushered us all to the other room. "Have a seat. I'll bring out the coffee cups, and we can discuss this whole kit-and-caboodle. It has to be hashed out. That's all there is to it."

"You're right, Grandma." I nodded at the detectives. "Sit down and Aaron can bring in more chairs. We have an awful lot to discuss here."

"Cookies, anyone?" Grandma asked.

"We're just fine, Mrs. Ott. A little confused but nothing else," Erlandsen answered.

"Don't tell me this has to do with Dolley Madison," Mergens said. "It's over two hundred years ago."

"So? There's plenty in history that's unanswered to this day. Sit." I pointed at the sofa. "We'll get started." Aaron brought in two chairs. When the men were seated, I said, "Let's begin with the sampler. The one on the wall. Have either of you two truly looked at it?"

"I suppose that we may as well start from the top once again," Erlandsen said.

Both detectives reached for their notepads.

"Hold on a minute." I glanced at Grandpa, who stood. "I'll be right back." I watched him go for the wall hanging and set it down on the table between us.

"Thank you." I was about to speak when Grandma entered with a plate of chocolate chip cookies and the full coffee cups. She set the tray down beside the framed sampler. "You boys must be hungry. Now, let's get started."

"Here," Grandma spoke to each individual as she passed the cups around. "Now listen to my granddaughter. She makes sense so keep your ears open."

"We don't like chewing our cud more than once, sonny, so remember that." Grandpa smiled at me.

"Let's hear it, Liv."

"Samplers? This must be what it is," Mergens said, looking at it. "Go through this all and pretend that we're kiddies."

"Here goes. You see these corner motifs? They mean something—but what? We're not sure." I pointed them out. "See? Now why is the flag in this corner? Any idea?" When they both shook their heads, I pointed to the side strawberries. "Why are there thirteen? Why thirteen seeds also on the individual strawberries?"

"No idea," Mergens said.

"How about you?" I glanced at Erlandsen who shook his head.

"All that comes to mind is the thirteen colonies," Mergens said.

"Bingo! I think you may have won this round." I smiled, and they both slightly chuckled. "Also, now look closer you two, the four strawberries along the short side, they have the thirteen seeds."

"So? Four on either side. Thirteen across the top and bottom." Mergens scratched his head. "Where's this getting us?"

"Moving on. We have also found out that at Alexander Hamilton's house in New York City. You must remember who he is?" I glanced at them both.

"You tell us," Erlandsen said. "We'll play along."

"He had been the first Secretary of the Treasury and was able to figure out how to tax the republic to pay our debts after the War of Independence. Remember the Whiskey Rebellion?" They looked at me like I'd lost my mind. "It's time for another history lesson. Hamilton is the person who was shot in the duel with Aaron Burr."

"Oh yeah! Now it's clearer. Go on," Erlandsen said.

"I'm sure. Never mind," Mergens said, grinning. "Go ahead."

"The Grange, as Hamilton's house is referred to, is original, as well as standing on its original property. There's a similar patterned sampler hung on a wall inside of the house. The corners are the same except for the odd one. The three corners have a marigold, but the upper left has a rose."

"The other three have marigolds? Like this?" Erlandsen sketched a picture on his pad. "It's odd. You're right."

"There's more to it than that." I pulled out my phone and brought up the image of the sampler from Montpelier. "Look. Tell me what you see."

"Oh my," Mergens whispered. "Another one, only not quite the same. Almost exact except for the corners again."

"Right. The fourth corner has the tombstone. From what I can tell, it says 'Polly'. Why on earth would she have her bird's name put on the tombstone unless she buried the bird there?"

"We've also wondered why the gadroon says, 'Polly'," interjected Aaron.

"I have yet to do much more research because there's always been something getting in my way, but now that these two thugs are out of the way. Maybe it's possible." I slid my phone on the table. "Now you see why we're curious about Dolley Madison?"

"The sampler is also from her hand, did you know that?" Grandma asked. "Bet you didn't."

"Nope." Erlandsen sipped his coffee after eating a bite of his cookie. "Very good."

"I knew they'd be appreciated," Grandma said, smiling.

"But how does this have anything to do with the murder?" Mergens asked. "Explain this to me. To us. How is it relevant?"

"The cufflinks," Grandpa stated. "Think about it. Polly imprinted around both. Polly? Now the tombstone—Polly? When will it end? All of these coincidences?"

"All these coincidences will add up to something, but the question is—what?" Aaron replaced his empty cup on the tray.

"The cufflinks are in the bank with the letter from Dolley bequeathing them to the Putnam family is right beside it," Grandpa said.

"You have the original letter, but didn't tell us?" Erlandsen said, knocking his forehead. "When will this end?"

"Keep going," Mergens stated.

"Montpelier Estate is anxious to get Grandpa's cufflinks to the museum. They plan to send the historian, Don Strowbridge, to fetch them, but he wants to make sure they're original. The handwriting original, etc. They want us to have our attorney present for the exchange."

"I plan to wear them during the wedding ceremony, so it's a bit dicey," Aaron said. "We'll need police backup."

"Duly noted." Erlandsen looked at me. "There's something else too, isn't there?"

"Yes. Besides the Putnam Family Bible. There are also letters here from Dolley." I gave them a minute to digest all the information. "Don't you see? It has to add up to the killer?"

"And the family secret, which Jackie mentioned to Liv," Aaron said.

"Ahh, the family secret. Whatever is imprinted on the gadroon will lead us to it. The clues on the sampler, with the cufflinks, must tell us what it is. The clues are in front of our face, but what is it? That's the mystery? What are we looking for? That's what we're after right now. The gadroon will tell us where it's located."

"That still doesn't tell us what the secret is," Erlandsen said.

"No, it doesn't. We have to decipher the clues," Aaron replied.

"I might be forced to rip off that turban of hers to get to the bottom of this," I stated.

"You'll figure it out, Liv. All in due time." Grandma looked at me. "I'm sorry for not telling about the bequeath letter sooner, but we didn't know about the other Dolley letters. I inherited them and they just came into my possession."

"I haven't scratched the surface with reading the letters." I leaned back, and wondered when this would end.

"Before we leave," Erlandsen said, "let's discuss what we do know about Dolley Madison from history. Not a whole lot between all of us."

"During the War of 1812, Dolley Madison was left alone in the White House while Mr. Madison, who is the final president to fight in a war during his time in office, was with his troops. The White House was virtually undefended. Dolley would periodically climb on the roof with her telescope to look for British troops. Several times she was told to leave the 'President's City' to avoid being captured. Finally, she entrusted her slave to help her load up personal items and, at the last minute, she made a quick decision to save George Washington's portrait. It's believed that that is the one on display in the White House. On her way out the door, she made sure that the table was set plus the prepared food was placed on the table. She hoped the British would be in a better temperament if they had a full stomach, but they burned the White House anyway. Dolley barely made it out of the city in time. She sent a letter to her sister. She liked people, had parties called 'squeezes' all the time and served good food. People loved her."

"We already know this." Mergens glanced around the room. "What in that leads you to believe that she's hid something?"

"A gut feeling plus the known clues." I clamped my jaw tight.

"There's really nothing to go on," Mergens said. "There's no firm conclusion that these are clues."

"Then why did Stone ask what's on the brooch?" Aaron asked.

"This is pie in the sky," Mergens said.

"Listen to me, Liv. If there is a killer out there, he'll slip up and we'll get him," Erlandsen said.

"I'm firm. You don't have the right people in custody."

"As it stands right now, we do have the two killers." Erlandsen looked at Aaron. "You are to stay out of this investigation and keep your fiancé out of it too."

"Yes, sir." Aaron looked straight ahead. "It's clear."

"I've left a message with the Montpelier security officer and he'll get back to me." Mergens stood. "Tell you what. We'll dig the best we can into this Madison stuff, or at least I will. It's outdated by some odd years, but I've always loved a good mystery."

"We'll continue searching for the suspects. But the cufflinks need to stay in the bank until the wedding. Armed guards will accompany you at all times the day of the ceremony. They'll be undercover. As far as picking up the estate representative, we'll take care of that. It's now top priority. We'll get the criminals, so don't worry." Detective Erlandsen stood.

"That's good news." Aaron stood. "I'll look after Liv. She won't leave my side. We'll stay out of the investigation."

"What's the motive for Jackie's murder?" I asked. "Do you have one?"

"No," Erlandsen shook his head. "Let's hear what you think."

"We don't know what we're after, but the killers are definitely greedy. They know there's a 'secret', but no one knows what it is," I said. "However, they have a strong suspicion that it's worth a fortune. I am in agreement."

"We'll keep digging," Mergens said.

"Combine the known clues with the gadroon, and we'll find the 'secret'. I'm positive." After moment of silence, I said, "The wedding is one week from now."

"We'll be in touch."

Once they'd left, we stared at each other. "What do we do now?" I wanted to know. "We can't just sit." I stood and placed my hands on my hips. "Let's sift through those letters again."

I left the room and brought both boxes of letters back and set them down on the coffee table.

"My dear, it's almost time for supper. What should we do?" Grandma asked.

"Order a pizza," Aaron said.

"Let's get started." I pulled out a stack of three letters, then set it to the side. "I hope they'll give us something to go on."

"They should. She always wrote letters. There must be volumes of them out there—somewhere," Aaron said. "Let's get started."

"I agree, but…" I shook my head, knowing I wasn't getting anyplace. "One sentence read 'brilliant idea, add symbolism,' and to 'hide it'. Another made reference to Polly, who I understand was her parakeet."

"Macaw."

"That bird's come up too many times, Olivia." Grandpa got up and left the room, returning with a cigar. "Puffing on a cigar helps me to think. Aaron, want one?"

"Sure. I'd never turn one of those down."

Grandpa claimed they were imported from a South American company, but I suspected that they were Cuban.

"Let's say, for the sake of argument, that the number thirteen stands for the colonies. I think we've already concluded that, right?" I began reciting the colonies, counting them off with my fingers. "Virginia, Maine…. You know? I'm looking them up so that I know the order. There's got to be significance in that."

"Love these," Grandpa said between puffs.

"That reeks. Can't you two go into the office?" Grandma pinched her nose. "You're gonna make me sick."

"August?" Aaron started moving to the office. "Coming?"

"No way. I'm staying. This is getting interesting." Grandpa smiled. "What's the fourth state?"

"Maryland." I stared at him a minute. "It could be the answer we're searching for, but the strawberries dance across the sampler. What is that supposed to mean?"

"One answer leads to more questions. It's never ending." Aaron puffed on the cigar.

"I'm sure glad they don't smoke those things very often." I passed out the unread letters, one to each. "Let's each read one out loud. Grandma, you start."

"All right, dear." She cleared her throat and began.

*"Dearest Mother,*
>*Sorry for not writing sooner, but I've been kept busy. The idea is fabulous, but you're confusing. Please don't worry so about me. I will write when I can. I have much to do and much to accomplish.*
>*Your loving son*
*John"*

"That's really rude." Grandma handed it back to me.

"Mr. Madison paid a lot of his debts and never told his wife. Dolley was totally unaware of her son's misfortunes. John rarely saw his mother." I said, "Grandpa." I nodded at him.

*"Dearest Jemmy,*
>*I've received one candle from Mrs. Adams. Do tell me how Martha is, and don't forget to bring me a candle which belongs to her. Maybe one which lights her way?*
>*Your loving wife,*
*Dolley"*

"The candle. Is it a clue?" I took the letter from him and set it with the other. "Aaron?"

*"Dearest Sister,*
    *What a brilliant idea. The soldiers adore it.*
    *Your loving sister,*
*Anna."*

Silence overtook us, as we each became lost in our thoughts. Aaron was the first to speak. "So now we have a reference to Abigail Adams and also Martha Washington."

"What's the significance of the candle?"

"Whatever it is, the soldiers adore it."

"Brilliant idea." Aaron puffed the cigar. "Confused her son. This has to add up to something, for sure."

"She made all that ice cream, you know." Grandma giggled. "She was the first to serve strawberry ice cream in the White House. Who couldn't resist ice cream?"

"And, the recipe is treasured? Why embroider samplers about ice cream?" I shook my head and stared up at the ceiling. "Grandma, it doesn't make sense. Ice cream?" I shook my head, and sighed. "It's probably just a secret about the ice cream."

# Chapter Twenty

After my grandparents went to bed, I cuddled into Aaron's shoulder.

"How're ya doin'?" He squeezed me tightly.

"I'm doin' all right, I guess." I looked up at him. "I wonder how the letters and candle fit into the clues?"

"Well, we'll have to think about that," Aaron said.

"And, piece them together," I said. "I hope the detectives find out something soon that will help us out."

"Me too." He kissed the top of my head. "I'm going back home, and hitting the sack. You're tired and need to do the same thing."

"You're right."

When Aaron left, I headed upstairs to bed. I fell asleep thinking about the letters and wondered if there might be copies of her handwriting at the History Center in St. Paul. I vowed to drive out there early the following morning to have a look for myself. Mikal had taught me a thing or two of what to look for when he analyzed my handwriting. Starts and stops. Wiggles in the lines. Dotting the letters or curly-cues.

Once morning came, I got up instantly. Grandma had left a note on the counter.

*A. Do you want to try out DM's ice cream?*
*B. Me buy the ingredients?*
*C. You buy it?*

I circled, *A.*

The second note read:

*Grandpa promised no more cigars in house.*
*Can he smoke at Aaron's?*

    *Yes.*

    *No.*

    *Maybe.*

I circled, *Maybe.*

The woman drove me crazy sometimes, I thought, giggling. I wrote a similar note only on a new page.

*I'm going to the History Center to look up DM's handwriting.*
*Can you go to the store?*

    *A. Yes*

    *B. No*

    *C. Call me?*

I headed out the door. I figured they were at breakfast with a bunch of friends. They were always busy.

The drive thru of my favorite coffee shop was open, so I purchased a roll and coffee to eat and drink while driving. I jumped onto the 94 Interstate, which brought me near the History Center. It didn't take long before I parked. I knew the way around and also several of the librarians and support staff since I'd spent many hours researching for my doctorate degree.

After taking the elevator to the correct floor, I stood in front of the help counter until my friend, Sandy, came over to me. "Hey, you! Long time no see. Whatcha been up to?"

"You wouldn't believe it if I told you." I grinned. "I'm kind of in a hurry. I only have about an hour until my store should open."

"What can I help you with?"

"Do you…" I held up my finger because my cell phone chirruped. I read the text. "Grandma's going to watch it for me. That's a relief."

"You're lucky to have her. I remember how much you talked about her." Sandy glanced over my shoulder. "I have to get busy."

"Oh." I noticed that a couple got in line behind me. "Do you have samples of Dolley Madison's handwriting? I sure hope so."

"That's right. You're a descendant, aren't you?" She thought a moment. "We do. I know exactly where too. Let me take care of this couple, then I'll get you set up."

"Thanks." I went to the nearest empty table to wait. I watched as she helped the couple before going into the back room.

"Right here." She brought over a book; opening it to the given pages. "It's not exactly easy reading because of ink and water stains. At least you'll have a pretty good idea of what it looked like."

"Thank you." When she'd left, I took the book and headed for a more secluded area. I looked around to make sure I was alone before removing the letters from my bag. I had brought two. One had the ice cream recipe while the other spoke of the candle.

*What is the equation? How does it fit together?*

Carefully I opened and closely studied them. The loops were identical as far as I could tell. The letter lines of her 'l's' flowed. Her signature seemed the same also. Further on, I compared her hand from later years, following the dates, and noted that the difference was a shaky appearance which fit the timeline. I was satisfied. Declaring it authentic was up to the authorities. At least now I could be positive, in my mind, that they were, which meant that I was on the right track.

But, right track for what? I was still clueless.

I brought the book back to Sandy, said "Thanks," and left.

I pondered stopping at the University library, and decided to since I had the time. I hadn't been to campus for a long time. It took forever to find a parking space, and just as long to walk over to the building. I knew where to find the books, so headed up the stairs—straight to the American History section. Two books about the War of 1812 and the Madison era stood on the shelf, which I brought over to a study carrel.

Before opening the first book, I sent messages to Aaron and Grandma, telling them what I was up to so they wouldn't worry.

Within seconds, they'd both answered back. Grandma was at the store with Grandpa while Aaron had gone to work.

My search started with the war and I skimmed through the pages, learning little. I continued skimming and covered the Federalist Papers. Little else was written except about how she'd used her spyglass and the soldiers, plus her slave to escape. There weren't any handwriting samples. I did learn a little about the siege of Fort McHenry and how the British blocked our seaports—commandeering our ships.

I went on to read about Dolley's life. She'd married at a young age to John Todd and they had two children—John Payne and William Temple. Yellow fever took both her husband's life and William's in 1793. Dolley married James Madison one year later. John Payne never married. I searched for Dolley's sister Anna Cutts. Anna, sister Anna's daughter, married Richard Cutts, and they purchased Dolley's house in Washington D.C. on Lafayette Square which is now a National Historic Landmark. James Madison purchased the house in 1828. When he died, Dolley held the mortgage. She had to sell Montpelier because John gambled and couldn't hold down a job. Dolley was destitute upon her death and very lonesome. John rarely corresponded or visited his mother.

*What did this new information mean?*

I closed it all out then headed back to my car after returning the books.

As I drove to the store, I thought over what I'd just read. From basic history classes. I settled on the thought that she'd buried Polly.

But, that was a stupid idea. Did she bury a candle that came from the former First Ladies, or had she melted a candle from each, only to later bury it? Why not just set it out in Montpelier and enjoy it? If she had, where is it? I found myself growing more confused. Soon, I parked behind the store right next to Grandpa's car.

Once I'd opened the back door, I called, "Grandma! I'm here!" I found Grandpa snoozing on a chair in the workroom. There was a note from Max stating that he'd be in touch, but he had errands to run. I dropped my purse and hustled out to the showroom.

"Busy?" I stood by the counter. "Any phone calls?"

"I've contacted our attorney, Mr. Nye. He'll be in touch with Montpelier," Grandma said.

"Oh, good. That was going to be my next question." I smiled. "He'll be here during the ceremony and make sure that we're covered legally, right?"

"Yes, after he's read what Don shows him."

"All the legal papers, you mean?" I questioned. "How's Grandpa taking it?"

"He's all right with it, really. Now we won't have to worry anymore. They'll be in the right place, where everyone can see them," Grandma said.

"Good." I glanced around the room. "Any customers?"

"Not yet. Dorrie called. She'll be here later."

"Good." I looked up at my First Lady pictures. "They look crooked. Traffic must cause the shifting," I concluded.

"Did you find out anything worthwhile? Anything that we don't already know, I mean?"

"The writing samples match the letters. I should give them to you to take home," I said.

"I'm not surprised. What's on the agenda for tomorrow?"

"Last minute things. Most people have been contacted, but there are only a few. We'll send out the five invitations. That'll make the guest list complete. I know we should've done it sooner, but there hasn't been time."

"Everyone's been called. This is more of a reminder." Grandma smiled at me. "We'll stop by the caterer to make sure that Ingrid is doing okay with the menu."

"Pastor Dahl hasn't been in contact. I'll give him a buzz." I slipped out my phone to call the church. After a few formalities, I said, "Okay, we'll see you at two. The wedding's at three." We disconnected. "What a mess. Planning a wedding around a murder and assaults."

"At least when you marry, you'll have Aaron to protect you."

"He already does."

"I hear Grandpa moving around back there. It's time for me to go," Grandma got up. "I'll let you know after I've seen Ingrid."

"Here, let me give you those letters." I followed her into the workroom, where we found Grandpa rubbing his eyes.

"Time to go?"

"I believe so." Grandma took the letters from me. "We'll be in touch. Take care now and be careful."

"I will. I promise."

After they'd left, I headed out to the computer to check my e-mail, where I found several to answer. After taking care of them, I logged onto the website and found two from prospective customers inquiring about prices, plus the individual houses. I answered the best that I could. The last on the list had me a little worried. It read: you're next. I quickly forwarded it to Detective Erlandsen plus sent him a text.

I decided to send a message to the Boston Historical Society to inquire if they knew of any correspondence between Dolley Madison and Frances Scott Key. I hoped for a quick answer. When finished, I got up and began to dust around the houses as well as to make sure that all the furnishings were in place. Every so often, I found a chair, doll, or lamp that had toppled over. I always blamed the shifting on the amount of traffic or because of the floor creaking. I looked up just as a young woman opened the door where she stood with the door wide open behind her.

"Hello. How may I help you?"

"I'm so interested in Michelle Obama and her thing and how she's so hip on things and everything. Oh! Just want to see the house that they're in now. You know? The White House? This is the right place, isn't it? The home of the White Houses?" She glanced across the room, and covered her mouth. "Oh, yes."

"Come in and have a look around." I hoped she'd close the door, as it was cold outside. "The houses over here are like what it's today. The White House, I mean." The woman already had me mixed up. "The house the Obamas live in."

"This place is wonderful. I must bring my grandma here plus my aunt," she counted her fingers, "then there's my cousin. I do have two sisters or is it three? Oh dear me, my mom just got remarried. My dad is going to also, but I don't know if he has any children."

I wondered if this woman had rocks for brains. "You take your time. Just look around at your own pace. I'll be right here if you have any questions." I walked away to let the young lady look on her own. My head was spinning from listening to her. It wasn't long before she asked me a question.

"Would you please come here?"

I walked over and looked at what she pointed at. "That's the Oval Office."

"Oh. Well. I think I better go, but I'm sure that I'll be back," she said.

"Thank you." Before going back to sit to catch my breath, I made sure that all was well and right inside the Obama White House.

I heard Dorrie and Max's voices as they entered through the back door. I got up and walked out to them. "Pshaw! You wouldn't believe the fast-talking young woman who just left. She took my breath away!"

"Glad it was you and not me." Dorrie chuckled.

"Tell me about last night," Max said. "Heard something about it on the radio."

"Wanda and Stone are in custody and I believe that they're being charged with murder." It still didn't seem right in my mind. "I'm not so sure about them."

"Why?" Max asked.

"Did they try and kill you too?" Dorrie's eyes opened wide. "I bet they're after the cufflinks. You still have them, don't you?"

"Yes, they're in a secure location. I don't want to talk about it." I looked at Max. "Something just doesn't seem right, but I'm not sure what it is, in answer to your question."

"I'm keeping an eye on you," Max replied.

"I'm going to push all this out of my mind for now. Tomorrow we'll send out the few invitations even though it's late. You both know you're invited, and you can each bring a date."

"Yep! Figured as much."

"Brad wondered about that, since I hadn't received an invitation yet." Dorrie grinned. "At least now we can plan."

"Plan for what?" That struck me as odd, but I ignored it.

"What to wear," Dorrie said.

"Oh, sure. By the way, would you two mind watching the store tomorrow? I should've asked sooner, but forgot because of all this other stuff going on."

"No problem. I can use the money," Dorrie answered.

"Sure. I'll be down to open up."

"Thanks," I said, relieved. "Dorrie, would you mind seeing to customers while I finish making sure that all my inventory is in shape? I could use time to sew up a dress also."

"Sure. How about if I put out more decorations?"

"Go ahead."

"I'm going to look through these heads that I ordered and get them lined up for carving. I also need to sharpen the knives," Max said.

I began my chores by opening the cabinet doors and taking out the inventory notebook. Since the first assault and so many pieces had broken, I'd had little time to make sure that my inventory was in place. The next hour flew past when suddenly, Dorrie pounded on the doorframe to get my attention.

"Yes?"

"A woman here wants to inquire about purchasing the Obama White House."

"Oh." I slid my chair back and followed her out to the showroom. The young woman from earlier stood, beaming like a Christmas tree and beside her was a small, older woman who reminded me of someone from Grimm's Fairy Tale.

"Hello again. How may I help you?"

"My granddaughter talked me into buying her a dollhouse for Christmas. This one here, I'll take it. How much?"

I gave her the price, and she cocked her head, as if counting all the pennies held in her bag.

"Can I talk you down about fifty bucks?"

"Sure." She seemed like such a nice little old lady and it was Christmas. She was probably on a fixed income. I would've loved one of these dollhouses as a present.

"It's a deal then."

"Go get Max," I told Dorrie. I turned back to the customer. "Let's get this written up while we wait for my employee to come and load it for you. Where's your car?"

"Right outside."

I glanced out, and my mouth dropped open. "The BMW?"

"Yep. Paid cash just last month. That's why I'm a little strapped."

"Okay. No problem. Tell your friends about this place for me, will you?" I rung up the bill and she paid the charges by counting out the cash from her bag.

"The Obama house," I told Max when he'd entered.

"I'll get right on it." He turned and headed back to the workroom, where I presumed he was going to box up a house. Dorrie followed.

"The boxes with all the items are on the top cabinet shelf," I called after her.

After all of the merchandise was carried out and the customers had left, we resumed our previous chores. The rest of the afternoon sped by without incident. I heard one or two other customers enter the store, but Dorrie took care of them.

As I counted items and made up boxes with furnishings for the various time periods, my mind wandered. Something still nagged at my mind, but I couldn't put my finger on it. Dorrie had said something a little odd also, which stood out. It almost seemed as if she'd expected a different outcome from last night's incident. Had she expected the two to kill me? Capture me? Then I wondered if I wasn't putting too much thought into what she'd said.

At the close of the day, I wanted to check for messages once again. I checked my phone messages and Detective Erlandsen had responded *"got it."* Aaron responded with, *"be careful."* I already knew that. I deleted both. At the computer I logged into my e-mail only to find several more messages that needed looking into. When that was completed, I checked the website mail and was happy that there weren't any messages. I was about to log off when a message popped on from the Boston Historical Society. It read:

> *Ms. Anderson,*
>> *As far as we can tell, there wasn't any communication between the First Lady and Mr. Key. Thank you for your inquiry.*
> *Mary Ann Olson, Director*

I replied with, a "*Thank you*" and shut down the computer. I felt as if I was back to square one.

## Chapter Twenty-one

The following morning was hectic, which gave me no time to dwell on murder. Grandma had me running around the house like the proverbial chicken with its head cut off, getting ready for the wedding. Even though the cleaning lady would come later, we had furniture rearranging to do, removing books from the shelves and dusting, plus counting and polishing the silverware.

As I sat polishing, which was dirty and boring work, I wondered where the set of silver had come from. I could tell by the heavy pieces that it was solid silver, with a Victorian design. The silverware chest was lined in soft blue fabric, but the amazing part of it was that there was a writing drawer under the chest. If my hands had not been filthy from the polishing, I would've slid open the drawer. Frankly, I'd forgotten about the drawer because I spent very little time in the dining room. It took a couple hours to finish polishing before I hustled to another job.

The next chore on the agenda was hand washing the chinaware. As I stood over the kitchen sink, I let my mind wander. I went back to the night before which brought my thoughts to Wanda and Stone. *Were they cold hearted enough to kill their boss? If so, then why? Why kill the hand that feeds you and signs your paychecks?* This train of thought left me puzzled and with more unanswerable questions. *Why didn't they know the location of the brooch?*

I stopped for a moment to give the store a call. Max was carrying out a vintage house and Dorrie had just finished ringing up the purchase. I said I'd call later.

Convinced that I needed to dig back into my memory for more clues, I started with Ronnie. That man was a bit crazy, taking all those pictures, and the stories he prints were usually only half-truths. I didn't think he was paid well, but he knew about the attic. Both Maggie and Ronnie had played up there when we were little bitty kids.

That led me to Dorrie. She obviously didn't get paid much but knew about the attic. Did that make her a killer? She'd known me since we were little kids too. Why would you want to hurt a classmate? It just didn't seem to ring true, but I still had that niggling feeling about what she'd said last night about Wanda and Stone. She used 'they' plus something else. What was it?

It took quite awhile before I'd finished washing and drying all the chinaware. When finished, I filled the teapot and turned on the flame. I called, "Grandma! Time for a break!" I walked from the room only to find her wiping office shelves.

"Grandma?"

"Got the kettle on?"

"Yep. I'm worn out." I motioned for her to follow. "I'll put on the teapot. You have a seat. It looks like we're both exhausted."

"Sounds good to me." She sat by the table while I reached for the cookie jar.

"Thanks. I'll make some sandwiches a little later."

While the hot water heated, I replaced the remaining items in the dish cabinet. I poured the tea when it was ready.

"Where's Grandpa and Aaron?" I wanted to know, because of my idea.

"Ice fishing." Grandma smiled at me. "It's a great way to get rid of the menfolk when there's plenty of cleaning to be done. They only get in the way."

I choked on my drink and coughed. When I'd composed myself, I laughed. "Grandma. You're hilarious sometimes."

"It's the truth. They'd be watching TV or eating, and you would have to work around them." She reached for a cookie and took a bite. "Mmm, good, even if I did bake them myself."

"Tell me your reasoning behind the murder."

"It's like this. Whoever is doing this must know about my connection to Dolley, right?" I studied her as I bit into a cookie. "Yummy."

"Our connection, Liv." Grandma nodded. "Continue."

"Jackie knew about the 'secret', which is a rumor, but we know nothing about it. Her employees must've known that also. Or, is the 'secret' a cherished but unknown fact?"

"What's your point, hon? We've been through all of this before." Grandma narrowed her eyes as she studied me over the rim of her teacup. She took a sip. "The two employees knew all about it, or else had an inkling. That's why they murdered Jackie. They also suspected that the cufflinks may be in the store, which explains the break-in. The motive was money and selfish reasons. Greed. Just like the Bible says, one of the seven deadly sins."

"Are you satisfied that it was the two employees?" I wasn't. Not by a long shot. I had to come up with a likely reason for them to return last night.

"If the police are satisfied, then we should be too." Grandma frowned. "Let's have this discussion when the boys return from fishing."

"Where'd they go?"

"Either Lake-of-the-Isles or Calhoun." Grandma finished her drink. "They wanted to stay nearby in case—"

"—of an emergency," I finished the sentence for her. "There have been too many lately, but they all circle around this house. That's what I'm getting at."

"You think on it, and we'll go over it later." Grandma stood. "Time to finish the kitchen. I've got lots to do before the big day."

The day drifted past while I spent the time thinking about my wedding and dreaming of becoming Mrs. Aaron Reynolds.

I'd finished the dishes, dusted all the books and shelves, and even dusted everything on top of the cabinets. It wore me out. I wondered how my two employees were doing in the store.

I gave Dorrie a call. "How're ya doin?"

"That darn Ronnie." I heard her sigh. "He thinks he's some kind of a detective. He wanted to know if I'd been up in your attic lately. Why would he say that? Brad told me not to talk to anyone."

"Brad? Hmm… what did he mean?" *That's odd about Brad. Was he part of this?*

"Because of the police and stuff," Dorrie tried to explain.

"We all did go to school together except Brad," I said, trying to needle her.

"I'm not talking anymore about the case," Dorrie said. "We're busy right now."

"Good." We disconnected.

*How odd. I only wanted to think about my wedding.* Not Brad or anyone else.

I was surprised I hadn't heard from Aaron by this time. It was five o'clock. I still didn't know where we were going on our honeymoon, which bothered me. I didn't know what to pack or buy. *Men!*

Grandma's heavenly smell of a pot roast with the trimmings, made my stomach growl. I went upstairs to shower, slipped into pants and a fresh top, and applied fresh makeup. By the time I'd finished dressing, Aaron and Grandpa were home.

I kissed Aaron, then set the table. Aaron went downstairs for a bottle of wine.

"Where are the light bulbs? The bulb's burned out." He came back up.

"Spares are down in the laundry room." Grandma set out the roast. "Better hurry, supper's ready."

"I'll help change it." Grandpa got up. He went after Aaron with a flashlight in his hand.

"Those two are like two peas in a pod." Grandma grinned, wincing when a speck of hot potato landed on her hand. "Ouch!"

I continued dragging out the needed items from the refrigerator and cabinets. Once all were placed on the table, I sat down.

The wine was poured, and by the time the guys had returned from the basement, I'd set the four full goblets down on the table.

"Glad that's done." Aaron sank into the chair beside me. His eyes sparkled when he gazed at me, which gave me a warm feeling. "You look like there's something deep going on up there. Let's hear it."

"About last night." I took a sip and waited to see if he'd say anything about it.

"Back to that again, eh?" Aaron offered up his glass, and said, "Let's toast to us."

We clinked our four glasses together and in unison said, "To us." We each sipped from our goblets.

"I've figured out a motive." I raised my chin with confidence as if I was an expert. "It's something really important that Dolley hid as kind of a *retirement fund*, to use a modern-day term." I glanced around the room, noticing that everyone looked at me with curiosity. "What would she have hidden? Suggestions?"

"What about the Federalist Papers?" Grandpa suggested. "It's what Madison wrote—laws and so forth for the Constitution." He shrugged. "Any better ideas?"

"The Federalist Papers were essays promoting the Constitution." Aaron took another swallow. "Surprised?" He grinned at me because my mouth had dropped open.

"Wow! I might make an historian out of you yet. Impressive. Any other ideas?"

"It couldn't be anything about her son, could it?" Grandma dished up the roast and then sat down. We started passing the food around and helping ourselves. "It has to be something simple. Why not the first draft of the Constitution?"

"I think we have it somewhere, like the Library of Congress or with the Declaration of Independence. Nice try but wrong. Sorry." I took a bite of the roast and soon gobbled my helping of it down. "Really good."

"What do we know?"

"All the clues are nameable except that we don't know how to tie them together." Aaron chewed on a bite of potatoes.

"We haven't had a chance to research the embroidery nor her handwriting." I took in a deep breath before continuing, "I swear, the letters are the key."

"We've read three of them together and you've read three others, but we can't seem to string a common thread." Aaron dished up another spoonful of carrots. "I think the key is with the gadroon, the imprint. Polly, where she's buried."

"Nope. It's gotta be the candle reference with the first two First Ladies that was in the letters," Grandma stated. She took her last bite and placed her dish over on the counter. "I say we finish eating, then reconvene in the office."

"Where we can analyze handwriting and embroidery." I swished my hair behind my ears. "We must compare the samplers. Maybe draw sketches of the known three." I glanced over at the dining room walk-through and remembered the silverware chest. "When was the last time you pulled out the drawer on the silverware chest?"

"About a hundred years ago. Why?" She looked perplexed. "Go ahead—take a look. No idea when I last looked in there. Don't think I've looked in it since my mother died. It was hers, you know?" She began clearing off the table, piling the dishes in the dishwasher. I helped by putting the food away and wiping off surfaces.

The men went into the office. I smelled the cigar smoke as soon as one was lit. I presumed Grandpa offered them. I realized that Aaron was developing the same habits as Grandpa, which meant that our lives would end up similar to theirs. They were happy, and my heart fluttered in response. We'd be happy also.

"I'm going into the dining room to see what's in the silver chest drawer. Want to come too?" I'd started for the doorway and waited. "Sure."

I stood in front of the chest, which sat perched upon the table-top. The chest belonged down inside on a buffet cabinet shelf, but since the wedding was next weekend, we'd left it out.

Grandma joined me in the dining room. "Here goes nothing." I flexed my fingers like safecrackers did in the movies before cracking open a safe. Slowly I began sliding out the two-inch deep drawer. Dust filtered in the air and I sneezed. The drawer slid hard, as if something was blocking its passage. I jerked it from side to side until finally it was completely opened, revealing an empty space. I wasn't exactly sure what to expect, but the cartoon characters of Tweedledee and Tweedledum came to mind. Ronnie had nicknamed me Tweedledum after the old English nursery rhyme characters when I'd almost failed ninth grade algebra.

"I'm so sorry, Olivia." Grandma wrapped her arms around me. "It's been so hard on you, and you had your hopes up high that you'd find the missing clue. Now there's nothing."

"I feel miserable," I frowned. "Let's go." Once I closed the drawer, we left right away for the office.

"What did you find?" Aaron questioned. Between his two fingers he held a lit cigar. He swiveled the computer monitor around for all to see as the two of us sat down on the settee.

"Nothing was inside the drawer." I shook my head, reached for a tissue to blow my nose. "One less place to concern ourselves with."

"Hon? You were hoping the answer was there, and then all this mess would disappear so we could get on with our lives, but it didn't happen." Aaron pointed out the flower prints that lined the computer screen. "We've done some research on embroidery, which shows we're right on about a Dolley connection. The Quakers used the same style of stitching. Marie's and Hamilton's appear to match the stitches from Montpelier."

"That's another score for our side." I blew my nose and leaned back in the settee to relax. "I've already confirmed that it's her handwriting. I know it's not authenticated, but we're onto something."

"And the rose?"

"Robert Burns, the Scottish Bard." I cocked my head, remembering reading it from English Lit. "Robert Burns' poem. *A Red, Red Rose.*"

Aaron punched in a few keys. "You're not going to believe this." His eyes lit up. "Burns' birthdate is January 25, 1759, and he died on July 21, 1796. The dates work. The publication of the poetry fits the Madison birthdates. Dolley easily could've owned a copy of his work."

"I'm not surprised. The pieces are coming together. But to what?"

"We have to find out about the brooch gadroon."

"It's time to wade through more letters." I went to get the letterboxes. Upon my return, I set them down on the small table. "Where are the six we already read?"

"I carefully stacked them. Now they're down in that rose cavity here on the desk," Grandpa said. "I showed Aaron how to get into it."

"Good place for them." I tended to think that it was a perfect place, since no one but the four of us knew of the hidden pocket. "Should we each read another letter aloud?" I opened the box, and drew out four more to pass around. "Who would like to go first?"

"First let me run home to fetch four sets of plastic gloves." Aaron jumped up from the office chair and was out the door within seconds.

While we waited, I picked up my cell phone to give Dorrie another call. "Hi. How did it go this afternoon?" She explained that two customers came to look at the dollhouses. One was interested in the Eisenhower, and the other, the Kennedy dollhouse. Before disconnecting, I said, "What about Ronnie?" Her reply left me speechless.

"Ronnie asked me about the two suspects, Tweedledee and Tweedledum."

Aaron returned just as I finished speaking.

"What did she say about Ronnie? I can't believe that he used to be nice," Grandma said.

"He never was nice. He'd bully everyone on the playground only to later make fun of them. When Mom and Dad were killed, he laughed. He'd make fun of my girlfriends and me when we'd play dress up, even though he liked wearing Daddy's old Marine Corps uniform. He was mean."

"It sounds like it. I daresay that not much has changed. Too bad," Grandma said. "Hazel, his mother, is a nice woman. She looks out for his daughter, Jessica. Don't forget, you have to see her for the final music arrangements."

"Did we ever get the bracelet back that Dorrie stole when I was about fourteen? Remember that?" I said.

"Yes, I do." She shook her head. "Not that I recall. Why?"

"Just wondering. I'm starting to think weird thoughts. Also, there's Brad, the chauffeur. He would've heard Jackie and Wanda talking in the limo about the family secret. I just wonder." I scratched my head. "I feel as if I'm missing something."

"Don't worry your pretty little head so much. It's your wedding. Everything will work out. Be happy. You're already beautiful." Grandma's eyes twinkled.

"Thanks." I kissed her and grabbed a set of plastic gloves from Aaron. He made sure we each had a pair before passing the next four letters out. "Grandma?" I wondered if she wanted to read hers first.

"Sure." With the letter in hand, she adjusted her eyeglasses to read it. "Here goes."

*Washington City,*
*Dearest Husband,*
   *Let's take a drive to visit our Williamsburg friends once I've returned from Montpelier. I believe that we need to visit the fair City for our Countrymen. They need to see their President and Mrs. President so they know that we weren't injured in the War.*
*Lovingly,*
*Dolley*

"Now we have a reference to Colonial Williamsburg. Isn't that interesting? We have the war, and then travel plans. I think we're finally making headway," Grandma said. "Don't you see? It's mapping out their life."

"Never thought of that." I raked my fingers through my hair then said, "Next?"

"I'll go." Grandpa cleared his throat while opening the envelope and removing the letter. "Hmm. I bet she means Jefferson here."

*Dear Thomas,*
> *Please send me a small candle from your darling wife, if you have*
> *one. I'd so like to have one to keep her memory alive in my heart.*
> *Burns bright the light*
> *Of the wickless candle*
> *Held upright and tight*
> *By the glow of Jesus' feet.*
*Your First Lady,*
*Dolley*

"How come she signed it that way?" Grandpa handed me back the letter and envelope. I placed the letter back inside and gave it to Aaron who already had Grandma's.

"Wickless candle?" I thought about the newest clue. "This is an enigma, isn't it? Jefferson was widowed when in office. At the time, James Madison was Secretary of State, so they were always at the White House. Dolley, being Dolley, assisted him with formal gatherings, thus he began to call her his First Lady. It was a prelude and training for what was to come, but Dolley played the part well." I turned to Aaron.

"This one seems almost lame." Aaron held up the letter.

*Dear Mrs. President,*
> *Here is the recipe which you requested for Oyster fritters.*

Aaron glanced up and said, "The rest is all ingredients." He placed the letter into the envelope and set it on the pile. "People did send her recipes, didn't they?"

"Yep. That's how she was able to build everyone's trust and assist her husband in passing the bills. She used her bipartisan skills to the nth degree." I opened my envelope and removed the letter. "This is weird."

*There is a thing*
*which in the night*
*Is seldom used*
*but in the light.*

*It serves the female*
*maiden crew*
*The ladies and*
*the good wives too.*

*They used to take it*
*by the hand*
*And then it would*
*uprightly stand.*

*And to a hole*
*they it apply*
*Where by its goodwill*
*it will die.*

*It spends, go out*
*But still within*
*It leaves its moisture*
*thick and thin.*

"This is one of the strangest things I've ever read." I gave it to Aaron. "What do you think?"

"I think it might be the answer we're looking for."

# Chapter Twenty-two

I stood in the middle of the showroom and spun in a slow circle. Dorrie had certainly decorated it properly, and all in good taste too, plus keeping with the ambiance of the White House. A small table had been assembled which held a facsimile to the National Tree outside on the lawn. Another small addition was the inside tree featuring the various branches of the armed forces, which kept in the spirit of the current White House occupants. The two displays were tasteful, and I admired how nicely they fit with the other decorations.

"Dolley, it's our secret. Did you bury Polly in a cemetery?" I leaned in closer to the Madison dolls in case a flash of knowledge might pass between us. "You're pretty tight-lipped." I took a deep breath. At the Wilson White House, I stopped to say, "I bet you two kept your share of secrets because of the President's illness."

I continued around the room adjusting dolls and furnishings, the front door opened and a customer entered. Short and plump, the woman reminded me of Mary Lincoln.

"Hello. How may I help you?"

"I'm interested in the war years during the Lincoln administration." She gave me that cherry pie smile. "You see, I impersonate the First Lady, and would love one of your houses."

"I thought you looked like Mrs. Lincoln." I smiled back. "Come right here." I waved her over. "This is the house you want to see."

"It's beautiful. She did a lovely job of decorating, didn't she?" She ooohed and ahhed. "Which room is the Lincoln bedroom?"

I pointed it out to her. "This room is where little Willy died."

"Oh my." I noticed tears filling her eyes. "I'll buy it."

"You take your time looking at it, while I get my helper to load the house for you. He's just in the back room." I began walking away, stopped to look back. "I'll be right back."

"Okay."

When I returned, she stood by the counter and I rang up the purchase. It wasn't long before Max emerged with the needed boxes while Dorrie entered with the rest. When they'd reentered, and we were alone, I said, "Thank you, you two."

"Anytime." Max grinned. "This place is starting to hop, isn't it?"

"Word is getting out," Dorrie said.

"You two will be able to take over when I leave for our honeymoon? Grandma can help out too."

"We'll be fine," Max replied. "Marie can bring some of her cookies."

"Next Saturday, you can close early so you can make it for the wedding. We sent the invitations over the weekend, so you should get them today. Kind of late, but, well—that's how it happened."

"We'll probably close at one," Dorrie stated. "I have to get dressed and so does Brad. He asked me to mention, that he'll be around if Aaron needs help with the tables or make sure that everything is safe and secure."

"Sure, I'll tell him." I drew in a deep breath and suddenly felt very tired. "I've got wedding errands to run, so I'm taking off. You'll be able to close up?" I glanced at Max.

"Will do. No problem."

"Thanks." I grabbed my bag, and slipped on my coat, heading out the door. Grandma texted me as I jumped into the car, asking me to meet her at Ingrid's, the caterer. I started the car, and began driving over the bridge down toward Hiawatha Avenue, eventually meeting with Ingrid.

We'd changed the menu a few times, eventually deciding on the original menu, along with a medley of cooked vegetables, plus two kinds of potatoes—twice baked and mashed—which had to be peeled, cooked and mashed by hand, plus an assortment of breads as well as pasta. Of course, there'd be melted butter and plenty of garlic in the scampi, since this was one of Aaron's favorite dishes. I wanted the menu to be all seafood, but Grandma rejected the idea because not everyone could eat it. There must be a variety, as she stated.

The week was a whirlwind of errands with the proverbial last minute planning. Few people were invited, but we had to meet with the police plus the attorney to make sure that the cufflinks transference went without a hitch. By Friday, I was a wreck and very happy that the wedding was only a day away.

Aaron and I decided to have a small dinner party the evening before the groom's dinner, the following night. We invited Dorrie, Brad, Maggie, and Tim for a small dinner at Aaron's house. I was giddy with excitement, but I also wanted to get a personal take on Brad.

When I heard Aaron's voice, I chased over to meet our guests at the door.

"Hi. Thanks for the invitation," Dorrie said, walking inside. "Have you met Brad? I think you have, Liv, but not Aaron."

"Glad to meet, ya." Brad thrust out his right arm. I couldn't help but notice the large disc earrings he wore, and around his neck was a heavy cross. I wondered why I hadn't noticed his jewelry the day he'd chauffeured Jackie, then realized he had worn a suit.

"We haven't really met. I only saw you opening and closing doors for Jackie." As I shook Brad's hand, I bit my lip instead of wincing. The man's grip was tighter and stronger than a lumberjack's. Standing dwarfed beside him, I felt like I was Little Orphan Annie and he was Paul Bunyan. "Come on in." We stepped aside, and at the same time, Maggie and Tim appeared in the doorway.

"Where's the beer?" Tim started for the kitchen.

"I'm right behind. Coming?" Aaron asked Brad.

"One more night remaining before we're married." It seemed like the right time to question Brad about Jackie. "Did Jackie ever complain in the limo?"

"Nope, I heard very little. There was a partition between me and the passenger compartment that she kept closed. I did hear something about jewelry. I haven't a clue what she was referring to."

"Jackie sure has me puzzled." I glanced at Maggie. I thought really hard, hoping for mental telepathy, that she wouldn't say anything.

"I wonder if she didn't mean the cufflinks that August wore on their anniversary?" Maggie giggled. "Remember that? We couldn't find him for the toast."

*Shoot! My telepathy didn't work.*

My heart sank to my knees, or at least felt like it. I found it hard to catch my breath. Fortunately, Aaron spoke up. "August was in the office behind closed doors smoking a cigar with his neighbor, Hank."

"Yes, they evidently made some kind of date or bet, that Grandma would leave Grandpa for Hank back in high school, since they were old school chums." I grinned, hoping that it would put an end to that vein of conversation.

"That's too funny." Maggie chuckled. "They adore each other."

"I saw those cufflinks. I was here for the anniversary party, so I remember them. They sparkled and shone like diamonds." Dorrie eyed me over her glass. "I bet they're worth a fortune. Aren't you wearing them, Aaron?"

"I could pay my student loans off," Brad said. "I suppose your cop buddies will be incognito during the ceremony?"

"No clue," Tim said.

*Bad vibes.*

"No idea where they are or what they're worth," Aaron said, looking at me.

I started talking about my wedding dress, getting the holiday finery tomorrow, setting up everything, and all the flowers we had ordered. I felt overwhelmed at all there was left to do, but both

Maggie and Dorrie volunteered their services. I had to remind Dorrie that I needed her in the store.

The wedding was planned for four o'clock with the reception immediately following. I glanced over at my house and realized that my grandparents were probably strolling through it, making sure that everything was in its place.

A rented movie brought an end to the evening with our guests exiting soon after it was over. I was satisfied knowing that Dorrie and Max would watch over the store in my absence the next two days.

It felt good to be alone once again with my honey, kissing each other as we climbed the stairs to his bedroom.

The morning brought sunshine and a promise of warmer temps, even a possible thawing. We both got up early, and went over to help my grandparents.

The day began with the caterer arriving with extra chairs and folding trays to scatter around the house, which Grandpa and Aaron supervised. Grandma busied herself making sure that everything was done to perfection.

"What are you looking at?" I stood beside her, staring at the vases of pink, red, and white roses on the dining room table.

"Trying to decide which vase to put where. They're so lovely. So very beautiful." She smiled, and gave me a big hug. "You're going to be very happy and make a lovely bride. I can tell."

We headed into the living room, arm in arm. The beautiful greenery and mistletoe hung over the doorways, combined with the added holiday decor took my breath away. It was all so lovely.

"Jessica's going to want to rehearse." I looked out the window and noticed that Grandpa and Aaron were positioning electrical cords to connect with angels, which lined the front sidewalk. "It's going to be so beautiful. I'm so glad that we're getting married here. Thank you."

"I wouldn't have it any other way," Grandma said.

The day flew by. The keyboard was positioned in the TV room, and the open bar was set up in the office. The dining room sparkled with the addition of draped Mini Lights circling the greenery. The caterer brought the cheesecakes. She returned several more times with pans and the food service warming cart, which was arranged near the kitchen table.

Jessica began rehearsing just as Maggie sent me a text message reading "*How r u do n.*" I sent one back, "*Go n crazy.*" I slipped the phone back into my pocket.

Once everything was set up in the yard, we went inside. We took turns getting ready for the evening's dinner. Grandpa was taking us to a new restaurant out in Burnsville, The Forest. The menu was quite pricey, but Grandpa was treating. We had a delightful meal—duck under glass, steak, trout—and of course I had to have lobster. Silly of me, I know, but I love it.

I spent the night with Aaron. I had a hair appointment in the morning. Aaron and another officer planned to accompany Mr. Nye when they drove to the airport to pick up Don from Montpelier.

"Busy day."

We kissed before going our separate ways.

At eight-thirty, Maggie messaged me, "*Car died u pik me up.*" I wasn't surprised. She always seemed to forget to shut off her headlights or else would get flat tires. The kids in her neighborhood were mischievous and would throw nails in the alleyway. I responded, "*Ok.*"

I quickly finished dressing. Maggie and I had not only booked hairstyling appointments, but also facials with makeup application. Our appointments would take all morning. Pictures started at two o'clock. It was already nine.

With my bag in hand, I chased out the door. I honked as I parked outside Maggie's house. In seconds, she was out the door and rushing toward the car.

"I'm so excited!" She slammed the car door shut. "Aren't you?"

"I'm ready to split." I was too. My heart leapt every time I thought of Aaron and taking the marriage vows.

I drove toward Forty-Second Avenue and Thirty-Eighth Street, parking behind Jeanette's Hairnet. I glanced at Maggie as I unbuckled my seatbelt.

"Time to get remade." I climbed from the car.

The morning zipped by, and I felt like a beauty queen after the facial. I loved the light-pink tones and soft blue shadow she'd given me. My hair was styled in a French braid with soft ringlets framing my face, which fell on my neck. My red hair sparkled under the sun that reflected in the mirror as she held it high for me to view the back.

"Thank you. It's lovely." I turned toward Maggie. Her style was much the same only without all the ringlets. Also, of course, not the red hair. "You're beautiful."

"You too. When Aaron kisses you, he'll never let you go."

"I hope so."

After paying, we drove toward my house, but I parked my car behind Aaron's, so Mr. Nye's driver could park in my spot. He'd soon arrive with Don, who hadn't arrived yet. I hoped there wasn't a problem. His flight was scheduled to arrive at ten; it was now noon. Just as I started walking across the lawn, a Cadillac parked in the street. The driver got out and opened the two side doors. I walked over to meet him while Maggie continued to the house.

"Hello," I said, and held out my hand once he'd climbed from the vehicle. "I'm Olivia Anderson, the person who contacted your offices."

"Oh yes. Liv."

"Don." We shook hands.

"I am excited to meet you in person, as well as your grandfather, especially since you may be the caretakers of the famous cufflinks." He smiled at me. "Where's your grandfather?"

The back door opened, allowing Grandpa to step out. "Olivia? Maggie's wondering where you are. Come on! You must get dressed."

"Oh, dear. He's just as nervous as I am." I chuckled.

"You're beautiful," Aaron whispered, and kissed me.

"Do you have the items?" I asked.

"They're right with me." Mr. Nye patted his briefcase. "We picked them up after we left the airport, then came right here. Where are the guards?"

"They're outside, keeping watch," Aaron said. "Brad showed up also, to make sure that the tables are set correctly. He's down in the basement retrieving another wine case. We'll keep it in the back entryway."

"I'm not sure that I like the idea of him being around."

"I'll be fine, Liv, he's a friend."

"I'm not convinced of that."

I tried to toss it from my mind as I hurried into the house.

It was now eleven and the photographer we had hired was due to arrive at one.

"Maggie!" Glancing around the meticulously decorated room, I marveled at its beauty. The wonderful scent of roses and pine filled the air. I took a deep breath, and smiled.

"Up here!"

I dashed up the stairs, knowing I'd find Maggie in my old bedroom. I burst inside, then we gave each other a big hug. "The big day! Finally!" We jumped up and down, holding each other.

"Next, it'll be me and Tim." Maggie smiled. "I hope, anyway."

"I'll make sure you get the bouquet when I throw it." I began removing my clothes. I snagged a ringlet, which caused me to wince. "Ouch."

Grandma's version of *Here Comes the Bride* echoed as she climbed the stairs. I peeked out before opening the door completely.

"Where are the men?"

"They're all over at Aaron's. The men will dress there. That's where Mr. Nye and Don will stay until the wedding begins." Grandma entered the room. "The two guards are with them. You might know who they are, since they work with Aaron and Tim."

"Good," Maggie said.

"Brad is here also, he's fetching the wine cases from the basement."

"Does he know the code for the cellar?" Maggie asked.

"I heard August giving it to him," Grandma said.

"I'm not sure how much to trust him, but there's nothing harmful about wine," I said, giggling.

"Is Aaron wearing the cufflink set throughout the ceremony or only for pictures?" Maggie asked.

I slipped my dress over my head, shimmying as Grandma helped pull it down.

"Throughout the ceremony, but he'll remove them immediately afterwards. Aaron will make an excuse to head for the bathroom, and someone will be with him at all times."

"Let me fasten your pearl buttons, and then Maggie can do the train." Grandma smiled at me and gave me a kiss. "You're as beautiful as your mother. She was lovely in this dress, but you're even lovelier." Tears filled her eyes. "I'm so proud of you." She choked back tears as she began fastening the buttons.

After Grandma finished my buttons, I helped Maggie into her dress. She looked gorgeous. The deep red fabric made her blue eyes look like the sky. Grandma scooted over and I zipped the back of her dress for her. Right up until picture taking time, we continued primping and fussing over each other.

I began singing *What a Wonderful World* but had forgotten some of the words. I thought of Mitch Miller and the bouncing ball. That tickle in the back of my mind began once again. When I started singing, *True Love*, by Bing Crosby, causing me to picture the bouncing ball, a smile crossed my lips, I felt as if I was on to something.

I knew I had to find Aaron if only to see those cufflinks.

Just before our photo session, I reached for Aaron's hands to hold them, which gave me a chance to stare at the cufflinks. The sapphires waved like a flag, the diamonds sparkled like stars, and there were thirteen that I counted on each one. The four ruby-red stripes reminded me of the four-sided strawberries on the samplers. I wanted to say something but didn't dare.

"I've got it." I pictured and thought of the bouncing strawberries and the four specifically placed motifs on each sampler. The flag on Grandma's sampler, stood for what? I thought of *The Star Spangled Banner*, when it was penned, and the history behind it. The flag waving after the fighting at Fort McHenry. Francis Scott Key witnessing the bombardment from inside of a Royal Navy ship in Chesapeake Bay during the Battle in the War of 1812. The rose stood for the love of our national anthem. I was uncertain what the fourth sampler corner meant. A tombstone? How strange. Or not? What was the third corner motif? A candle? The wickless candle had to symbolize the passing from one president to another. Or what else? Passing of the torch? It didn't make sense, but I knew I was heading in the right direction for solving the 'secret' mystery.

"You're not gonna believe this," I whispered. My heart almost beat out of my chest when I kissed him. "Don't forget to ask Don what's written on the brooch gadroon."

"I will, babe." Aaron wrapped his arms around me.

"And, show him the letters."

"Gotcha."

The photographer took several more pictures.

Jessica started playing Beethoven's *Ode to Joy*. Dorrie and Brad seated themselves. Mikal arrived. Max arrived with a girlfriend—and they all sat near the front. The other guests were arriving, and before long the seats were filled. I looked around for the two guards, and finally spotted them. Mr. Nye and Don weren't in view, so I suspected that they were still at Aaron's. Grandma took her seat which gave Jessica a cue to begin the prelude to *The Wedding March*. Aaron and Tim stepped up to the front.

My heart skipped, causing me to lean into Grandpa, who took my arm and cradled me like a baby girl. Maggie, Grandpa, and I stepped outside, and *The Wedding March* began.

The ceremony happened quickly, and we were soon presented as husband and wife. An undercover guard cajoled Aaron to leave. Aaron chuckled and smiled before disappearing.

During those few minutes without Aaron, I hurried to the bathroom to refresh my makeup. My grandparents greeted guests, and made sure they were comfortable and had something to eat and drink.

When Aaron returned, he whispered, "Everything matched. I gave them the letters. But he wouldn't tell me what was on the gadroon."

"Darn it. But now I know. I've got it figured out." We laughed and hugged. "Let's go meet our guests."

Grandma and Grandpa were still milling around, greeting everyone. A few people had found their way over to the refreshment bar, or were waiting in line. When Dorrie came through the line, she whispered that she was unwell but Brad wanted to eat before leaving. The motion of the Cadillac leaving the curb caught my attention as I glanced through the window. I was relieved that the cufflinks and letters would soon be in the museum where everyone could enjoy viewing them.

The caterer and her helpers were busy with the final dinner preparations as Aaron and I wandered near. Since the champagne for the toast was cooling, we each had a glass of wine. When the caterer was ready to serve, she signaled us and we all found our tables. Pastor Dahl said a prayer, and we began to line up at the buffet table.

The wedding guests stayed well into the night. When the guests were gone and Aaron and I were getting ready to leave for our motel, Grandpa hollered upstairs to us. As I'd slipped out of my dress and hung it on the hanger, Aaron said, "Better find out what he wants."

"I suppose." I stuck my head out the door. "What's up? It's midnight. We want to get going."

"Let's have a glass of champagne before you leave."

"Good grief," I moaned under my breath. "Okay," I hollered down to him.

"We'll satisfy them, then head over to our house to grab what we need."

I wanted to club Aaron for agreeing to the delay in our departure for the motel. But I did pick up on his reference to "our house." I kissed him before following him out the door. Down in the living room, Grandma and Grandpa each sat in a chair.

"You two look so good together." Grandma got up to give me a hug.

"Let's have another toast to your happiness before you two love birds sneak away." Grandpa's eyes were moist, causing me to feel happy and sad at the same time.

"Okay, but I'll take down dirty towels first."

I scooted away to the kitchen to pick up the towels. I flipped the light switch for the stairway, but the light didn't come on. I wondered about that, since it was recently replaced and I shivered. *Something wasn't right. I could feel it.*

The stairs creaked, and I could've sworn that I heard a chair scrape.

"Hello?" I tentatively called. "Anyone here?" I found that the bulb for the light at the foot of the stairs was also burned out.

The back of my neck got cold and my heart started beating faster. Quickly, I headed toward the laundry room to drop off the towels. I heard another scraping noise as I walked across the cement floor. A faint vanilla scent made me gasp. I picked up a bottle and threw it toward the scent. The bottle smashed into a million pieces. The deafening noise echoed in my ears, but then I heard someone chuckle softly. I was not alone.

"Who's here?" It suddenly occurred to me who the mastermind of this whole situation was, Brad. Because of the excitement, also not being in direct contact with him, I hadn't smelled vanilla. Now, I realize that he'd been the person who had entered the house, spilled out all the jewelry and murdered Jackie for the cufflinks. I began moving backward. Another floor scrape. Glass crunched underfoot, so I stopped. I trembled from the top of my head to my toenails. Suddenly, he snapped on a flashlight and shot the beam over me. I noticed he stood near a chair, and in his other hand was a huge gun, the size of a cannon, aimed right at me.

"Get over here. Right now," he said. "I've waited all day. I've searched your house, combed the attic. Collected odd jewelry to sell from the cache in your grandma's room. The cufflinks are here. Give them to me."

"Was Dorrie in on this, too?"

"No. Hand them over, and I'll leave."

"Yes, sir." I raised my arm and threw the towels in his direction. He pulled the trigger, but I'd successfully ducked. I shouted, "Aaron!"

"Sit." Brad motioned me over with the gun. "One more time and you won't be so lucky." When I was within arm's reach, he dragged me over, plunking me down into a chair. "Tell me where the cufflinks are." He started wrapping tape around my wrists, taping them against the chair arms. "Start talking, Liv."

"You think we have them? Then you're dumber than I thought." He snarled at me.

"You're not getting anything else out of me." I clamped my mouth shut tight and shook my head.

"Where are they?" Brad slapped my face. "Tell me. You dumb bitch. You have any idea how much those are worth on the open market? All our loans paid. We could live comfortably for the rest of our lives!" He towered over me while holding the gun to my forehead. "Talk." He slapped me again, but this time my nose bled.

"They're gone!"

"Lady! Talk!"

"No way." I closed my eyes and tried to figure a way out of this situation. As he leaned over to anchor my ankles to the chair with the tape, I raised my knee, catching him in the groin. When he dropped the gun, I was able to kick it further away. As he grabbed my leg, I caught his shirtsleeve with my mouth, biting him. He hollered, "Ouch!" and tried stepping back. I thought my teeth would come out of my mouth. "You're going to pay for this!" He backhanded me. At the same time, I heard my name being called. "Watch out! He's got a gun!"

Grandpa clicked his flashlight on while Aaron jumped for the gun. I'd kicked it far enough so it wasn't within Brad's easy reach. Aaron held the gun steady on Brad and said, "You're not going to dodge it this time. Should've known it was you." My gutsy Grandma reached up and screwed in the loose bulb, lighting up the room. Aaron stood near the storage shelves that lined the wall near the dryer, keeping the gun pointed at Brad.

"I've called for backup and an ambulance. Not that I care about him." Grandpa stared at Brad. "You'll pay dearly for this, sonny." He growled under his breath before clenching his jaw tight.

I focused on the gun that Aaron was aiming at Brad.

"Let's talk this through," Brad softly said, backing toward the laundry sink. "We can work this out. Hand over the cufflinks, then I'll leave."

"You're dumber than I thought," Grandpa said.

"I've got to untie Liv," Grandma started for me.

"Stay where you are," Aaron said. "The police will soon be here."

I figured Brad was heading for the jugs of laundry detergent. I watched as his eyes darted from one corner of the room to another. It all happened so quickly that it's hard to remember in what order things occurred, but Brad lurched at Aaron. Aaron pulled the trigger which wounded Brad in the shoulder. I was scared out of my wits when Aaron shot a second time, nicking Brad's arm and causing him to double over in pain.

"You okay, honey?" Aaron looked at me with glazed eyes.

"I'm fine, baby. Untie my wrists."

As soon as I was free, I looked down at Brad, and asked, "What do you know about the family 'secret'?"

"I thought the cufflinks are the 'secret'," Brad answered, wincing in pain.

"You idiot," Aaron said. "What were you planning on doing? Holding the first person hostage who came down the stairs?"

"Nope. Tie up Liv, and get the cufflinks. I figured Grandpa must have them hidden."

"You didn't find them," Aaron said. "Dorrie played you for a fool."

"I told you she didn't have anything to do with this." Brad glanced from Aaron to me.

"The police will get to the bottom of this," Aaron said.

"You're stupid," I said, and almost kicked him, but I raised my chin and marched out of the room, going right up the stairs. *The cufflinks are part of the 'secret'.* I was in the living room when the police entered. Behind the uniformed policemen, in walked the two detectives, Erlandsen and Mergens. I pointed toward the basement. When Detective Erlandsen asked me what kind of gun it was, I said, "Very big, about the size of a Civil War cannon."

I slumped on the couch with Grandma right beside me. It took the police another two hours before they left, and we knew that they'd be back the following day.

Along with all of the excitement of the wedding and the events in the basement, the tea made me sleepy, but I couldn't sleep. The image that I kept seeing was the barrel of a Civil War cannon, aimed right between my eyes.

# Chapter Twenty-three

When the airplane descended onto the tarmac, I held my breath and clutched Aaron's hand. Reagan National airport was finally coming into view and, as I peered out the window of the jet, I could see the Washington Monument and Capitol building. The plane circled and the aerial view of all the magnificent monuments was breathtaking.

After disembarking, we wound our way past all the checkpoints and searches, strode toward the baggage handling area, and retrieved our luggage. My personal suitcase stood out like a sore thumb. It had a U.S. flag on one side, and I'd plastered a picture of Dolley on the other.

Don had arranged for a chauffeur to meet us at the airport. He drove us to the Montpelier estate, two hours south of Washington D.C. It was two days since our adventure in the basement.

When we arrived at the estate we were directed to the museum, where the rubies, brooch, and cufflinks were displayed beside Dolley's red empire waist dress.

"It's lovely." I could barely speak, and needed to keep pinching myself just to make sure that I was alive, and hadn't died and gone to heaven. "What does the gadroon inscription on the brooch say?"

"I'll tell you in a minute. Right this way," Don escorted us down the hallway and into his office. His large oak desk filled half the room and floor to ceiling bookcases surrounded him. Aaron and I took the offered chairs while Don walked around, sitting in his oversized desk chair. He gave us a smile and said, "Williamsburg."

"I knew it." My eyes lit up. "We researched Bruton Parish Church at Colonial Williamsburg when it came up in one of the letters. That's where *The Star Spangled Banner* manuscript is hidden." My breath caught in my throat. "The rose signifies the song. It's loved by all."

"Explain all the clues to me. I'm puzzled," Don said.

"Here goes—I think, that the flag represents *The Star Spangled Banner*, the rose is a symbol for love of it. The gadroon, Polly, has me a little stymied, but it must be the name on the tombstone. The tombstone and the letters point to Williamsburg and Bruton Parish since it's been a congregation from the beginning of our American journey. The candle signifies the passing of the torch, I believe, but am not sure." I smiled. "That's my interpretation of the combined clues."

"Your interpretation at the moment," Don said.

"Correct."

"Honey, we have to find it first." Aaron winked at me. "We'll take a quick tour here before continuing to Colonial Williamsburg."

"Dolley was an amazing woman. Who's to say that she didn't do that? There's the copy with the music and one without. How do we know that she didn't receive the first copy directly from Mr. Key? She was so well-loved that it's quite possible." Don gave me a smile as he handed me the necessary legal papers for signing over the letters. "I believe the letters are authentic."

"I thought so." My palms were moist as I signed my name. The pair of cufflinks were already legalized. "Have you heard of a wickless candle once belonging to Dolley?"

"Sorry, but, no," Don said. "Can't help you out."

The tour of the estate was magnificent. We strolled past the well where Dolley had drawn cool water for making her fresh lemonade, and where she used to churn her heavenly strawberry ice cream. The Temple, with its view of the Blue Ridge Mountains, was breathtakingly magnificent. It is said that the Temple is where

Mr. Madison drafted the Federalist Papers, which led to the design of our Constitution. We visited the graves of James and Dolley Madison, the nearby slave cemetery, and walked along Dolley's flowerbeds, which were all covered with compost for the winter.

The mansion tour was all that I hoped for. In Dolley's chamber, I pictured her before her mirror, brushing her lovely brown hair. Her maid would've helped her dress, drawing in her corsets. We saw where she had served afternoon teas out on the porch. The mansion was so elegant but yet so welcoming, just like the lady of the house. Dolley's charm and wit still triumphed. I could feel her in every room and hall where we walked.

When the tour was completed, a chauffeur drove us to a car rental business, where a car was ready for us, and we headed for Colonial Williamsburg.

"Okay, read me that poem again, all the way through." Aaron drove onto the freeway. "The one about a candle." He glanced at me, smiling.

"Oh, sure, give me a sec." I reached into my bag and pulled out the copy I'd brought along. "Here goes." I read it aloud to him.

"Interesting," Aaron said, grinning. "The third corner of the sampler has to be a candle."

"I thought so too." I gave him a puzzled look. "First on the agenda is to explore the graveyard at Bruton Parish."

"This is fun." Aaron merged with traffic. "Dolley could get people to do anything for her. Trying to solve this mystery is fun, and here we are doing her bidding over almost two centuries later. I'm enjoying every minute, even if we come up empty handed." I took out my cell phone and began taking scenery pictures to send to Grandma. "Our reservations are for three nights at the Williamsburg Lodge. What a great honeymoon." I leaned over to give him a kiss.

"Yeah. I'd like to see everything, including College of William and Mary. Imagine that. All those buildings are preserved. Aren't we lucky?"

"Yes, very. John D. Rockefeller Jr. sure helped out with the preservation." I took a few more pictures of the buildings and towns, all decorated for the season. "The Bruton Parish rector and an attorney who is representing us should be waiting when we get there. There probably will also be a guard to make sure that the manuscript is safe, if we do find it." I slipped my phone into my pocket. Shivers raced up and down my spine. "We're on the right track. I can feel it."

"I think so too. Something that precious would have to be guarded," he agreed. "I'm looking forward to the two of us being alone."

"Me too." I took a deep breath. "My heart is pumping like never before." I held out my hands and stared at them. "They're shaking. Look at that."

After driving a couple of hours down to the Williamsburg area, we parked in the lot and checked into the hotel. I slipped out my cell phone and dialed the attorney and parish rector to let them know we'd arrived. We picked up maps of the historical preserve area, then went back out into the snow-covered streets.

"I can't believe that we're walking where the greats had once walked. And we can eat where they did too," I said, completely awestruck to see the doors hung with wreaths of fruit and greenery. A few houses had candles in the windows. "I'm all tingly inside. Let's look at the map and head straight to the church."

"Yep. We need to find the Duke of Gloucester Street." He turned the map around.

"It's right down here, just a couple blocks away."

Hurrying, we brushed past pedestrians dressed in period clothes. A corner group of impersonators sang favored holiday carols of the period. An impersonator of Thomas Jefferson was addressing a group of tourists. I knew that I'd eventually have to return and listen to the words of that brilliant man. Doors of some of the shops stood open behind him, allowing the sun to warm up their rooms, in spite of the winter chill in the air. The thatched-roofed houses were quaint and well preserved, as were the wood homes. Coming closer to the parish, we stopped to take in the site and noticed the armored car parked out front.

"Isn't it interesting that this brick Episcopal Church has been in continuous use since before the Revolution?" I sucked in my breath and stared at the church's tall wooden spire. "It's still just as active as ever."

"Let's walk around to the cemetery." Aaron led the way. "Fortunately, the gravestones are taller than the snow. We'll be able to read most of them."

"Yes, I see that. Everyone is here already." I began searching for the headstone that read *Polly*. "You look on the other side."

"Sure." Aaron began walking toward the newer-looking headstones.

Slowly, I walked up and down the rows of chipped, washed-out stones that had little or no visible writing left on them. Many were covered with moss, and I tried to brush them clean. Back in a corner, near the base of the church, was a very small stone that almost caused me to trip. Bending down, I noticed that it had an odd, circular design on it, like an oil lantern. With my fingers, I carved out the dirt, exposing the stone that read, 'Polly'.

"Aaron! Come here!"

"Coming!" he answered. "With the attorney, guard, and minister."

I knelt in front of the stone and continued swiping away the dirt, and Aaron knelt beside me. We tenderly finished removing the dirt and sediment as the three looked on.

"I think we've found the right stone." I looked up to the men. "It'll be just a matter of time until we find the manuscript. The manuscript's hidden in this church. This was the final clue given on the samplers."

"I'm from the office of H. Wyeth and Sons," the attorney said. "Mr. Henry. We'll take care of the details, if we truly find the manuscript."

"I'm the rector," the other man said. He cleared his throat. "Reverend Hancock."

"And I'm a guard from Williamsburg."

We all shook hands.

"Nice to meet you three." I was ready to jump out of my skin from excitement. "We're almost done cleaning the headstone, as you can see."

"Look." Aaron stepped aside, exposing the image of a candle.

"The candle. We must look inside for one." I stood up, and took a deep breath to calm my nerves. "Ever hear of a really, *really*, old candle that's been in the church since like *forever*?"

"That's odd, isn't it? I never noticed this way back in the corner," Reverend Hancock said, peering down at the stone. "Let me think a minute." He cleared his throat. "I've heard tales about the two First Ladies melting their special presidential candles together, molding them as one and then having it placed here in the church."

"An old candle, you say? Interesting." Mr. Wyeth shoved his glasses further on his nose. "Oh my. That would mean Washington and Adams, right?"

"A letter stated that Dolley melted a candle from Martha's estate, Abigail's, and Jefferson's." I shivered down to my toes. "There's four samplers, each with a different corner motif, which glue the clues together as one. The fourth corner is the tombstone exposing the candle. We must find it."

"Several letters indicated a candle," Aaron said.

"Let's go inside and see if we can figure this out," I said.

"I've kept someone in the sanctuary the past few days. I haven't wanted anyone to come in here alone, ever since receiving your phone call." Reverend Hancock led them to the main door and we followed him inside. "Let's all have a seat." He flipped on the lights. "There. That's better."

The beauty of the magnificent altar, draped in ferns and candles, took my breath away. Aaron squeezed my hand as we sank into the nearest boxed pew. Our mouths were agape as we looked around at the rosette windows on one side and sash on the other. The oak wood flooring looked brand new. The boxed pews kept the drafts from opened windows from reaching the congregation. A special canopied chair on a platform near the altar was still in position from when the governor, Spotswood, attended services in the early 1700s. A succession of galleries lined the walls with exterior staircases, designed for students from the College of William and Mary.

"The poem read something about a wickless candle at Jesus's feet. I don't see one, but I'm sure that it'd be small in comparison to an altar candle." I glanced at the reverend. "Maybe we should climb up to the gallery and look down? We'd get a better perspective."

"I'm trying to remember." Reverend Hancock ran his fingers through his hair. "There's a very old candle, but where?" Hancock got up. "I think I know. It's not on the altar anymore." He started walking toward the stairs. "You're right. Let's sit up in one of the galleries."

"What about by the pump organ?" I followed him. "Have you seen a sampler at all? Hanging somewhere? Ever?"

"Sampler? Why, yes, of course. There used to be one hanging upstairs. Let's go take a look. You're kidding about the candles, aren't you?" Mr. Wyeth followed Aaron, who was close beside me. "A candle from the First Ladies?" He furrowed his brow. "I wonder if there was one?"

"We'll find out." Hancock led them up the narrow staircase. "Let's all have a seat, please."

"Smell that old varnish? Look over at the organ. It's gorgeous. It looks like a statue up there, hanging on a wall." I pointed to it. "Do you mind? Aaron? Come with me, you guys try and find a candle from here."

Aaron and I slowly made our way down the stairs, briskly walked over to the organ stairs, and climbed them.

"All these stairs are a pain," Aaron said, reaching the gallery.

"Look at that organ. It must be as old as the building. Wow. It's dated 1768. Living history." I gawked at it, and lightly touched it. "My heart is ready to stop beating, this is such an honor."

"The rocket's red glare, hon. Back to the moment."

"Yeah, the bombs bursting in air." I sank onto the bench with Aaron beside me. "It's here. I can feel it." I slowly glanced around the small room. *Dolley. Speak to me.* I tightly closed my eyes. "Where is it?" I pictured Dolley moving around and holding a long, narrow package. She stopped in front of a statue. "There's a small statue on the wall there behind the bench seat. You'd better go and get the others."

As Aaron left to call down to them, I lowered my head in silent prayer, offering devotions of thankfulness for the life of Dolley Madison, and gave a silent thank you for my grandparents. The voices and footsteps of the approaching men caused me to open my eyes.

"Ready, Liv?" Aaron returned from the top of the stairs and massaged my shoulders.

"I can't begin to tell you guys how nervous and excited I am." I glanced at each of them. "Let's say a prayer. Reverend?"

"Took the words right out of my mouth." We all bowed our heads. "Thank you, Lord, for helping this lady to locate the most exciting song in all our history. Amen."

"You mean the most spectacular." I corrected him before turning to raise the bench lid, and lifted out a four-inch diameter beeswax candle. Tears streamed from my eyes as I held it up to the light. "Just like the poem. No wick. Wickless." I turned it over and read the carved out letter *P*. "The corner motif was to lead us where her bird, Polly, was buried. The First Ladies candle, I figured is inside."

"Isn't this amazing?" Aaron blurted. He beamed.

"Exactly. A bird and the dancing ball. And now the wickless candle." I wanted to dance until dawn. "I saw Mitch Miller's Sing-Along videos, and thought of the strawberries along edge of the samplers, which Dolley had embroidered. The four strawberries were symbolic of Maryland, our fourth state. The dancing hinted at a tune, which led me to Frances Scott Key who was the most famous of American composers at that time."

"Polly? Samplers? Wickless candle?" Mr. Wyeth shook his head. "I don't get it."

"Her bird's name was Polly and the P proves it's the candle we are looking for." I pointed to it.

"You're connecting this find to a parakeet?" The guard shook his head. "Nothing makes sense."

"It will if this proves right." Aaron shot me a smile the size of the Montana sky.

"Aaron, do you have your pocketknife?"

"Here." Aaron removed it from his pocket, opened it, and handed it over. "Careful."

With trembling fingers, I began carving at the base of the candle, when a two-inch round block of beeswax dropped out. Carefully, I tipped the candle sideways and peered inside.

"Oh, my God. Aaron, you do it." My eyes opened wide and it felt like my heart had leapt into my chest.

"Nope, it's all yours." Aaron pushed it back.

I carefully extracted a copper tube from inside the candle. Tilting it slightly I poked my finger inside and gently pulled out a tightly rolled yellowed sheet of parchment paper. I painstakingly unrolled it, revealing the original copy of Star Spangled Banner by Francis Scott Key.

"I feel light headed and about ready to faint. I can't believe this." Silently I read it through moist eyes, before holding it up for the men to read.

"All this time it's been here?" Reverend Hancock asked, in disbelief.

"The clues led us here. The bottom was sealed with beeswax." I grinned. "That's my girl, Dolley."

"Wow," we said in unison.

"This is glorious," said Mr. Wyeth.

"Let's sing the last two lines before we give this paper to the guard, shall we?"

Immediately, we began singing,

*And the Star-Spangled Banner in triumph shall wave
O'er the land of the free and the home of the brave!*"

## THE END

## Author's Note

The copy of *The Star Spangled Banner* that Francis Scott Key wrote is on display at the Maryland Historical Society. There is also another copy at the Library of Congress. It is my understanding that it is not known which of these is the exact first copy of the beloved anthem.

The Banner is on display at the Smithsonian Institute.

I used the liberty of my imagination to fit the circumstances. The First Lady candle, samplers, and letters are all fictitious.

# About Barbara Schlichting

Barbara Schlichting was born and raised in Minneapolis and graduated from Theodore Roosevelt high school in 1970. She and her husband moved their family to Bemidji, Minnesota, in 1979. She attended Bemidji State University where she earned her undergraduate and graduate degrees in elementary education and special education. Ms Schlichting has been married for forty-four years and has two grown sons who have blessed her with five grandchildren and one great grandson.

## About This Book

The typeface in this book is 11.5 Garamond and Helvetica (for the headings). It was laid out using Adobe InDesign software and converted to PDF for uploading to the printing facility.

## About Darkhouse Books

Darkhouse Books is dedicated to publishing entertaining fiction, primarily in the mystery and science fiction field. Darkhouse Books is located in Niles, California, an inadvertently-preserved, 120 year old, one-sided, railtown, forty miles from San Francisco. Further information may be obtained by visiting our website at www.darkhousebooks.com.

CPSIA information can be obtained
at www.ICGtesting.com
Printed in the USA
FFOW04n2056140716
25908FF